Proust
in Black

Proust au noir

Proust au noir

Los Angeles: A Proustian Fiction
Fanny Daubigny
Translated by Bruce Whiteman

Hyperbole Books, a San Diego State University Press Imprint

Proust in Black, Los Angeles: A Proustian Fic-tion by Fanny Daubigny, is a translation of *Proust au Noir* (2019) by Bruce Whiteman and Fanny Daubigny and is published by Hyperbole Books, an imprint of San Diego State University Press.

San Diego State University Press and Hyperbole Books publi-cations may be purchased at discount for educational, business, or sales promotional use. For information write SDSU Press, San Diego, California 92182-6020

A special thanks to SDSU Press Editorial Associate Stewart Parker who served as executive copy-editor on this volume.

hype.sdsu.edu | sdsupress.sdsu.edu |
facebook.com/sdsu.press

Cover and Book Design by Guillermo Nericcio García,
memogr@phics designcasa

Regular Color Edition
ISBN-13: 978-1-938537-85-1
ISBN-10: 1-938537-85-8

FIRST EDITION PRINTED IN THE UNITED STATES OF AMERICA

The time has come to give up on civilization and its enlightenment.

Georges Bataille

At night, I lie.

Alain Bashung

For Guilhem and Adrien

Table of Contents

Prologue

The man who meditates not, lives in blindness; the man who meditates, lives in darkness. The choice between darkness and darkness—that is all we have.

Victor Hugo[1]

[...] true books must be the product not of daylight and chitchat but of darkness and silence.

Marcel Proust[2]

Black wrath. The wrath of Achilles.[3]

Black magic. Magic of our nights beneath a full moon.

Black light. The black of Pierre Soulages.[4]

Cobalt black, coal-black, ivory-black, blue-black, turquoise-black, grey-black.

Black that is filthy, nostalgic, death-bearing, terrifying, strange, brutal.[5]

---

[1] Victor Hugo, *William Shakespeare*, trans. Melville B. Anderson (London: Routledge, [1905]), p. 137.

[2] Marcel Proust, *Finding Time Again*, trans. Ian Patterson (New York: Penguin Books, 2002), p. 206.

[3] The story of Agmemnon's carrying off of the captured Briseis, thus provoking Achilles' wrath, is an important episode in the Trojan War in Homer's *Iliad*.

[4] This refers to the French painter Pierre Soulages for whom "light comes from blackness."

[5] The *Dictionnaire Littré*, a standard French dictionary first published in the nineteenth century, records the following: "Noir-bleu," a species of hummingbird; "Noir-brouillard," a brown or light-brown sandpiper; "Noir-manteau," a species of seagull; "Noir-brun," a species of goby (fish); "Noir-veiné," a species of agaric (mushroom).

How to get a feeling for the color black without being drawn into the black hole of its history? French scholar Michel Pastoureau did pioneer work.[6] This essay proposes a different story. A black legend of the color black. The alternative history of a color that is not just primary but also complementary, which becomes the commonalty in two heterogeneous artistic elements: cinema and literature. Film noir (American) and a closeted noir novel (French), Marcel Proust's *In Search of Lost Time*.

Nothing brings them together, and yet little separates them.

figure 1: Billy Wilder, Double Indemnity, *1944*

A city unites them: Los Angeles.

---

[6] Michel Pastoureau, *Black: The History of a Color*, trans. Jody Gladding (Princeton: Princeton University Press, 2009).

Los Angeles, fractal city. City on the fault-line, city at fault and in breakdown. A megalopolis with a complex geology.

In Search of Lost Time, fractal novel that seesaws between two centuries, the nineteenth and the twentieth.[7] A literary genre with a disputed chronology.

Film noir. A genre with a contested history.[8] From the beginning, film noir developed outside of the usual categories. If for some critics it seems to have roots in European detective fiction, for others its true beginnings lie somewhere in the hazy origins of Hollywood silent movies of the 1930s.[9] A singular visual birth in troubled waters.

But whatever its origin—disputed or verified—film noir always presents a single multivariate equation: a crime, a more or less shady detective, and a femme fatale.

In Marcel Proust's novel, *In Search of Lost Time*, the same equation is established but the crime is a symbolic one. And the murders happen one after the other. As the chronicle of the demise of an author, of a noble class, of a France that is feudal, monarchical, Catholic and rural, *In Search* also proposes an investigation. An investigation necessarily *black*. A novel with a complex cartography.

Where chronology, geology, genealogy, and cartography coalesce in overlapping ways in the same story, this essay is the result. An essay that is experimental by nature. Situated at the crossroads of literary history, visual arts history, photography and intellectual fiction, the essay which follows takes as its starting-point a re-

---

[7] Antoine Compagnon, *Proust: Between Two Centuries*, trans. Richard E. Goodkin (New York: Columbia University Press, 1992).
[8] Thomas Pillard, "Une histoire oubliée: la genèse française du terme 'film noir' dans les années 1930 et ses implications transnationales," *Transatlantica* (online) 1, 2012, uploaded December 14, 2012, accessed November 19, 2015. URL http://transatlantica.revues.org/5742.
[9] German directors who were exiled to Hollywood in the 1930s brought with them an Expressionist aesthetic which can be found in American noir films in that and subsequent periods.

reading of Proust's book as a *noir* novel which will serve as the basis for the script for a film noir.

figure 2: Howard Hawks, The Big Sleep, *1946*

For to write is to investigate, and to investigate is to write. For Proust, it was writing to the point of death, for his bed would be his final writing-desk, while for Marlowe it was investigating at the cost of his own life. To write and to investigate so as not to fall into *The Big Sleep* of consciousness.[10]

---

[10] The reference is to Howard Hawks's 1946 film, *The Big Sleep*.

In this literary investigation of a new type, it will be especially important to solve four equations in which the unknown quantities are called conscience, truth, desire and modernity. Four equations set out in four chapters whose common denominator will be a narrator assuming the role of a private detective—a constant in the story who, looking back, gives coherence to a whole that otherwise would be ever shifting.

While Chapter 1 explores the world of insomniacs and sleepless nights as the scene/moment of the crime in both film noir and Proust's novel, Chapter 2 examines the question of truth and proposes an arsenal of techniques and procedures for arriving at it. Chapter 3 considers the danger presented by the femme fatale through the pairing of desire/truth and how it constitutes the perfect framing of the crime.

Chapter 4 contemplates the aesthetics of fear, part of the privileged poetics of both film noir and the Proustian novel. From the fear of confinement to the tragedy of the war, *In Search* suggests that at the heart of World War I exists a singular collection of *little cabinets of horrors*, as American film noir will later, after World War II and at the dawn of nuclear war.

This essay frames a history that is as much about color as literary influence. From the almost inarticulate beginnings of film noir in Europe in the 1920s with the German Expressionist cinema to the modern American and French versions in the period from the 40s to the 70s, the investigation will cross from the deep black of the silent era to the blue black of contemporary productions. From Fritz Lang to Howard Hawks with a nod to David Lynch, film noir, even in color films, continues to take a somber view of things.

...you worked in bed,
like Marcel Proust.

-Who's he?
-A French writer.

So, each chapter will suggest a kind of double investigation, a literary version that will echo the cinematic one and vice versa. The detective novel as a supplement to film noir and film noir as a supplement to the detective novel.[11] And in this investigation of a new genre, the Proustian novel will be read as the poetic epicenter of a theoretical disaster, my research functioning against the grain of a certain kind of university discourse, revealing numerous fault lines between fictional discourse and academic commentary.

One last word of caution in reading the essay which follows: most of the films examined in this essay are American and were shot in Los Angeles, largely in the 40s and 50s when the genre was at its height.

Why Los Angeles? Well, because Los Angeles is the perfect city of crime, of the *noir*. It also happens to be the city where I have long lived and which abides in me. And as the painter Elstir (Marcel Proust's alter ego in *In Search of Lost Time*) puts it, one should not paint what you know but what you see. *To one's only desire.*

In short, this essay proposes a brief archaeology of the *noir* of a book open to the heart of an open city.[12]

figure 3, 4 opposite: Howard Hawks, The Big Sleep, *1946*
figure 5: next page: Angel's flight, LAX @2016 fdaubigny

---

[11] Film as a supplement, i.e. the way it can reveal what is not obvious in the text. The screen's whiteness which illuminates the text's blackness, in short. "Supplement" is understood here also in Derrida's sense of the term. See *his Of Grammatology*, trans. Gayatri Chakravorty Spivak (Baltimore: Johns Hopkins University Press, 1976).
[12] The reference is to Roberto Rossellini's film *Rome, Ville Ouverte* [Rome, Open City], 1945.

Chapter 1: White Nights

> *A sleeping man holds in a circle around him the sequence of the hours, the order of the years and worlds.*[13]
>
> Marcel Proust

In calling up the night, it is often the myths and folklore of childhood that are evoked. From the depths of the woods where the orphan gets lost to the grains of sand of the *Tales of Hoffmann*, the slow dive into the world of dream, whether terrifying or calming, brings back those long-ago stories read, at evening, in a window-seat; whether true or invented, stories that stay with us for a single night or a whole lifetime.[14]

In sleep, a bit of childhood is regained. From its first experience of sleep, the adult gives way surreptitiously to the child who, staying awake during the day, night after night enjoys again the pleasure or the pain, the unconscious and collective enactment of the archetypes of his or her own culture. Totems and taboos while the well-behaved sleep tight at night.[15]

Two years ago, when the 150th anniversary of the publication of Lewis Carroll's masterpiece, *Alice in Wonderland*, was celebrated, nostalgia for a world of dreams had never been stronger, even in a world of widespread insomnia in which Alice's given name reminds us of the name of an illness and a syndrome (Alice in Wonderland Syndrome).[16]

When the word "day" becomes identified with "productivity," "night" reclaims a space of resistance, removed from the demands of industrial production and consumption. Rest becomes again a

---

[13] Marcel Proust, *Swann's Way*, trans. Lydia Davis (New York: Penguin Books, 2002), p. 5.
[14] E.T.A.Hoffmann, *The Tales of Hoffmann* (Harmondsworth: Penguin Books, 1982).
[15] Bruno Bettelheim, *The Uses of Enchantment: The Meaning and Importance of Fairy Tales* (New York: Vintage, 1977).
[16] Lewis Carroll, "Life, What Is It But a Dream?" in *Through the Looking-Glass and What Alice Found There* (London: Macmillan, 1871).

little island of idleness, this peninsula of indolence that refreshes anyone overtired from staying up late:

> In the depersonalization of slumber, the sleeper inhabits a world in common, a shared enactment of withdrawal from the calamitous nullity and waste of 24/7 praxis. [...] Sleep is a remission, a release from "the constant continuity" of all the threads in which one is enmeshed while waking.[17]

Calling up the night is also to summon the treasures of the history of the French language which demonstrate the close connection, the link between insomnia and writing. From dark anger to black magic, from the brief respite of orgasm to the sleep of the warrior, from Achilles'[18] weakness to Voltaire's rage,[19] throughout the centuries the blackness of night has known how to share intimate space with the writer's white page.

To evoke the night, to speak of something sought for at the end of night, is in the end to speak of a major work of French literature, Marcel Proust's *In Search of Lost Time*, a text that stages an utterly commonplace story: a man sleeps, he wakes up, then he goes back to sleep.

Would Sleeping Beauty have become a man at the onset of the 20th Century?[20]

If in life the sleep of Marcel Proust was fragile and interrupted by serious bouts of asthma which forced him to shut himself up in a darkened cork-lined room, the narrator's sleep in *In Search of Lost Time* is equally fragile. The opening pages of the novel show us into the room of a man struggling with insomnia:

---

[17] Jonathan Crary, *24/7: Late Capitalism and the Ends of Sleep* (London: Verso, 2014), p.126.

[18] Jean Racine, *Iphigénie*, Act IV, scene 1: "Dans un lâche sommeil crois-tu qu'enseveli/Achille aura pour elle impunément pâli?" [In a cowardly sleep do you think that buried/Achilles will have gone pale for her with impunity?]

[19] Voltaire, *Triumvirat*, Act IV, Scene 4: "Sommeil! Sommeil de mort! favorise ma rage!" [Sleep! Sleep of death! Give me strength in my rage!]

[20] Jean-Yves Tadié, *Le Lac Inconnu: Entre Proust et Freud* (Paris: Gallimard, 2012).

> For a long time, I went to bed early. Sometimes, my can-
> dle scarcely out, my eyes would close so quickly that I did
> not have time to say to myself: "I'm falling asleep." And,
> half an hour later, the thought that it was time to try to
> sleep would wake me; I wanted to put down the book I
> thought I still had in my hands and blow out my light; I
> had not ceased while sleeping to form reflections on what
> I had just read, but these reflections had taken a rather
> peculiar turn; it seemed to me that I myself was what the
> book was talking about: a church, a quartet, the rivalry
> between François I and Charles V.[21]

At once the reader asks himself a question. *Why bother reading a novel in which nothing happens, in which one goes to sleep, both literally and figuratively?*

But in fact the time of falling asleep in Proust is far from an insig-nificant act; rather it is the time of drama *par excellence*. Few writers before him had dared to write about it. The instability of sleep creates a situation that is dramatic, rich, and complex for the dangerous shoals, shifting sands, and reefs of consciousness re-fashioned by sleep. So many risky moments by which the reader, if he does not stay alert, risks being sucked down and even running aground.

Is reality nothing but a dream?

Noir #1: *Sherlock Jr.* (Buster Keaton, 1924)

Not long after Marcel Proust leapt into the eternal night of the big sleep (the writer died on November 21, 1922), in 1924 Buster Keaton directed at MGM Studios a feature film entitled Sherlock Jr. *In this silent film the central character, played by Keaton himself, is a pro-fessional projectionist. But he aspires to become a detective. A rejected lover in his own life, the projectionist is in love with a beau-tiful heiress, and he witnesses the theft of a watch belonging to the young woman's father. The thief takes flight. Back in his projection room and drowsy from studying a guide for learning how to be a de-tective, the young aspirant falls asleep as the reel of film unspools.*

---

[21] Proust, *Swann's Way*, p. 3.

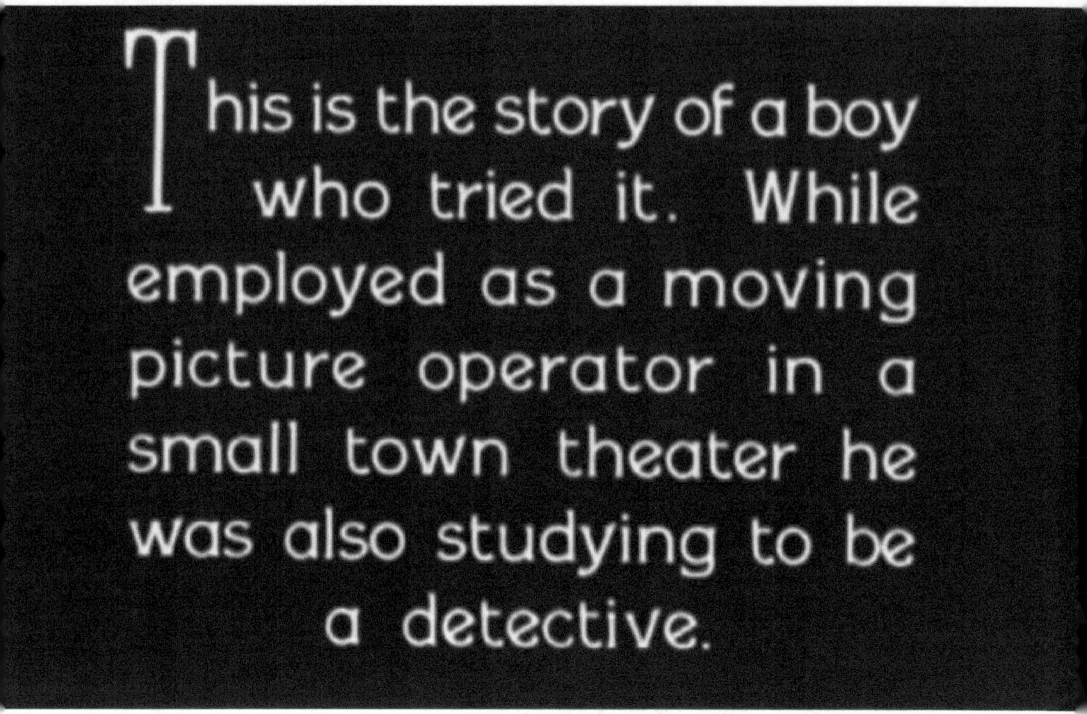

> This is the story of a boy who tried it. While employed as a moving picture operator in a small town theater he was also studying to be a detective.

figure 6: Sherlock, Jr., *Buster Keaton, 1924*

As the projectionist is plunged into a deep sleep, the crime plot of the film projected on screen mimics with a confusing precision the actual crime committed a few hours earlier, which he witnessed. But thanks to the film detective's cleverness, the guilty man is quickly overwhelmed. For the detective on screen is none other than the projectionist himself, Buster Keaton! Fiction and reality, then, are melded, and the dream world illuminates what reality makes dark. With Proust as with Keaton, a sleeping man is twice valuable. He holds in a circle around him the sequence of the hours, of the years and of intrigue.

figure 7: Sherlock, Jr.; *Buster Keaton, 1924*

If the imagery of the darkened room and with it that of the magic lantern is what probably best links the Proustian novel with the experience of film, Proust's relationship to film remains all the same quite ambivalent. While the aesthetics of *In Search* are broadly underpinned by the visual arts (photographs of the grand-mother, impressionist seascapes by Elstir, Combray's magic lantern), the writer views film more as an artistic practice which tends to suppress the essential link between sensation and memory, producing from reality "a series of residues largely the same for everyone."

> An hour is not just an hour, it is a vessel full of perfumes, sounds, plans and atmospheres. What we call reality is a certain relationship between these sensations and the memories which surround us simultaneously—a rela-tionship which is suppressed in a simple cinematographic vision, which actually moves further

away from truth the more it professes to be confined to
it. [...]

But that was not all. If reality were a kind of residue of
experience, more or less identical for everybody, because
when we talk about bad weather, a war, a cab-stand, a
brightly lit restaurant, a garden in flower, everybody
knows what we mean, if reality were just that, then no
doubt some sort of cinematographic film image of things
would be enough and "style" and "literature" which de-
parted from their simple data would be an artificial
irrelevance. But was this reality what reality was?[22]

All the same, Proust's resistance towards film was not a total and
definitive rejection, despite what the critics have made of it. The
objection brought by Proust against "the seventh art" weighs in
fact more against a cinema of realism which presents little more
than a flat and one-dimensional image of reality, a bit like the image of a literature of note-taking which contrives only to describe
things superficially, as, for example, with the Frères Goncourt,
whose style Proust abhorred.[23]

For the narrator of *In Search*, the challenge above all is to resist the
fate of "the bachelors of art" who fail to transcribe and to clarify
the hidden link between a feeling and a memory. In contrast to the
obscurity of stereotypes both literary and visual, Proust stands for
a cinema of intimacy that would develop and illuminate the great
black book of interiority. The writer's scale of colors and shadows
would be better allied with the aesthetics of silent black and white
film, a cinematic writing style in the 1920s something of a work in
progress, and subject to a jejune and feeble light that could illuminate only intermittently.

In Proust's preference for a cinema of intimacy, there is otherwise
the representation of an aesthetics of persistence of memory
against oblivion, reminiscent of Pasolini's "disappearance of the
fireflies": an art taken to be an act of resistance against an economy

---

[22] Marcel Proust, *Finding Time Again*, trans. Ian Patterson (London: Penguin
Books, 2003), pp. 197-198.
[23] Proust's narrator considers the writing of the Goncourts a literature of "mere
note-taking."

of *waste*, the final stage of production in a capitalist society, which indefatigably transforms the diverse into the same, the individual into the whole, and silence into noise.

> Friendship is a beautiful thing. The night I'm speaking to you about, we had dinner in Palermo, after which, on a moonless night, we climbed towards Pieve del Pino, we saw a huge number of fireflies, which formed thickets of fire in the thick bushes, and we envied them because they loved each other. [...]
>
> Thus were we that night. Afterwards we clambered on the sides of hills, between the brambles, that were dead yet seemed alive in their death, we crossed through woods and cherry orchards where the trees were full of fruit, and we reached a high crest. From there we could clearly see two faraway and savage projectors, mechanical eyes that were impossible to avoid, until at last we were seized by the horror of being found out, as dogs went on barking, and we felt guilty, we fled along the spine, the crest of the hill. [...]
>
> At the beginning of the 1960s, because of air pollution and, above all in the country, because of water pollution (azure streams and limpid canals), the fireflies began to disappear. When it happened it was like a thunderstorm. In a few years there were no fireflies left. Today, it's a very touching memory from the past.[24]

Pier Paolo Pasolini, who was also a devoted reader of *In Search*, here takes up again to his own personal and aesthetic account the *chiaroscuro* of Proustian desire. The fireflies cast a weak light on the ambivalences of desire against the blinding stupefaction and control of the projectors/censors.

The same struggle against the blinding of the machines existed with the actor Charlie Chaplin, a contemporary of Proust and Keaton, who in a speech entitled "Against the Talkies," spoke against the birth in his time of a film industry which he felt would do little

---

[24] Georges Didi-Huberman, *Survivance des lucioles* (Paris : Éditions de Minuit, 2009), p. 16. (Trans. Bruce Whiteman).

more than crudely and unimaginatively record reality and would transform it too into *waste.*

For the American comedian, the arrival of talking films would destroy the ancient art of pantomime by turning film into grotesque spoken theater. "Talkies," as he put it, "you might say I loathe them! They have come along to spoil the most ancient art in the world, the art of pantomime. They utterly destroy the great beauty of silence."[25]

For Chaplin as for Proust, works of art should remain the products of silence, of which the artist alone is the translator. Caught between two centuries,[26] between two traditions, the one ancient and the other modern, the actor and the writer are already acutely conscious that modernity's train is in motion and that only by maintaining the tightrope walker's art—away from the lights of power—can they reconcile these contradictions.[27]

Let us not forget that it is precisely with the figure of a tightrope walker that *In Search* comes to a close, with the image of a man staggering, upright on stilts, who in his final balancing act tries to go on holding onto a circle "of hours, years, and centuries around him."

> I finally understood why the Duc de Guermantes, who had caused me to wonder, seeing him sitting on a chair, how he could have aged so little when he had so many more years that I had below him, had, the moment he rose and tried to stand upright, wavered on trembling legs, like those of some ancient archbishop whose metal crucifix is the only solid thing about him, and towards whom hasten a few strapping young seminarists, and could not move forward without shaking like a leaf, on the scarcely manageable summit of his eighty-three years, as if all men are perched on top of living stilts which never stop growing, sometimes becoming taller than church steeples, until eventually they make walking

---

[25] "Against the 'Talkies'," *Los Angeles Times Annual Review* (1928), p. 121.
[26] Antoine Compagnon, *Proust entre deux siècles* (Paris : Seuil, 2013).
[27] The body of the clown is as it were cut in two: the posture is aristocratic, upright, and conservative like the white cane; the behind is disconnected, undisciplined, exuberant as a gang of revolutionaries.

difficult and dangerous, and down from which, all of a sudden, they fall.[28]

With Proust, the art of the tightrope walker is the consummate art of the sleepwalker.

If a line of cinematic inheritance in which the world of silence and night is equivalent to resistance can be traced from Chaplin to Pasolini, sleep, before being a subversive political act, is first and foremost, at the end of the nineteenth century when Proust begins to draft his novel, a question of public health.

When Proust evokes in his letters the occurrence of annoying sounds that prevented him from sleeping or woke him up too early, his remark gives us an intimate view of the fashions of urban life in the Paris of the 1890s.

In a letter of September 14, 1896, addressed to his mother, Proust essentially moans to himself about the state of sleeplessness that prevented him from working: "But I have to admit that because the painters woke me up early, I was forced to take a dose of Trional (80 milligrams), since I could not continue on so little sleep."[29] Recourse to sleeping pills, antidepressants, and anti-histamines is naturally a thing familiar to the writer's biographers, who see a strong link between the real-life insomnia of the author and the fictional one of the narrator.

Let us add that Marcel Proust's father, Adrien Proust, was a doctor and holder of the Chair of Public Health in the Faculty of Medicine at the Sorbonne, and that he was deeply interested in the revolutionary contributions of Jean-Pierre Charcot and Pierre Janet to sleep studies and the split consciousness which develops during this period. Without doubt, the novelist had access from an early age to his father's library and became aware of the work of these two men. Biographers are also more or less certain that he will have read *Le Sommeil et les rêves* [Sleep and Dreams] by Alfred Maury (1865) and *Le Monde des rêves* [The World of Dreams] by Max Simon (1888), while it is not likely that before his death he

---

[28] Proust, *Finding Time Again*, p. 357.
[29] Dominique Mabin, *Le Sommeil de Proust* (Paris : PUF, 1992), p. 69.

had read Sigmund Freud's *L'Interprétation des rêves* [The Interpretation of Dreams], which was not published in French until 1926.[30]

Through the experiments of Charcot, Simon, and Maury, sleep then reveals a complex reality, showing traces of an alternative culture in the hollows of a *cultural malaise.*[31] The question excited both scientific researchers and artists, who could see in hypnotically induced sleep a means of gaining access to a parallel subversive reality. And besides, Proust would not be the only writer to be swallowed up in the hypnotic abysses of sleep, since an entire generation of poets, including Gérard de Nerval and Charles Baudelaire, would explore in their work the shadowy zones of a modern culture which persistently celebrated the lights of the fairy electricity.

NOIR #2: *The Cabinet of Dr. Caligari* (Robert Wiene, 1920)

In German director Robert Wiene's Expressionist masterpiece, The Cabinet of Dr. Caligari *(1920), the plot focuses on the investigation of a horrible crime that disturbs the normal calm of the village of Holstenwall. By the end, the criminal is arrested and we realize that Dr. Caligari and his sleepwalking "puppet" Cesare, who is subjected to regular bouts of hypnosis, are in fact the perpetrators of murder.*

---

[30] Sigmund Freud, *L'Interprétation des rêves* (Paris: Myerson, 1926).
[31] Sigmund Freud, *Civilization and Its Discontents,* trans. Joan Riviere (London: Hogarth Press, 1957). The French translation of Freud's book is *Le Malaise dans la civilisation,* trans. Aline Weill (Paris: Éditions Payot & Rivages, 2010).

figure 8: The Cabinet of Dr. Caligari, *Robert Wiene, 1920*

Beyond just its beautiful black and white cinematography, Wiene's film skillfully demonstrates the tight connections that bind film, sleep research, and hypnosis at a time of questions raised by the Proustian novel. The film also shows beyond measure how the cinema, that magic art par excellence, is not just a machine for making dreams but can also produce the darkest crimes.

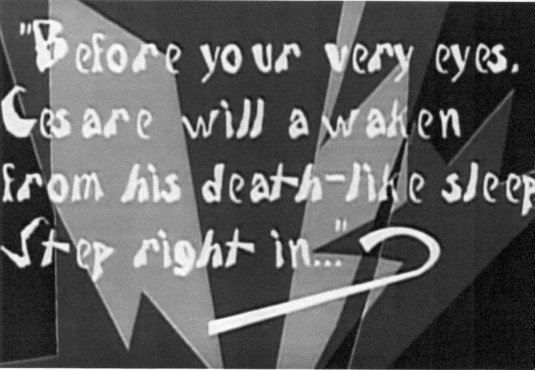

figure 9: The Cabinet of Dr. Caligari, *Robert Wiene, 1920*

Like Dr. Caligari, the writer Marcel Proust performed under hypnosis. And in the grip of his creator, doubly a creation god, the narrator of *In Search* is transformed into a serial killer. Needless to say, in Proust's world, the crime remains symbolic. It is a question of slaying time in order to more effectively revive it.

In the Proustian darkened room (a hotel room, an artist's studio, or a cabinet of curiosities), the narrator of *In Search* is at work deciphering time's book of magic spells which, in the middle of chaos, contains the secret of the perfect analogy and hides the secret of the world within its covers. With Proust, the artist is like a sorcerer's apprentice in the thrall of hypnosis, or like an alchemist who transmutes the mud of time into art.

When the writer Michel Butor describes Proust's seven rooms, he is referring with precision to the basic principles of alchemy which traditionally connect seven metals to the seven planets: Gold/Sun, Silver/Moon, Quicksilver/Mercury, Lead/Saturn, Tin/Jupiter, Iron/Mars, and Copper/Venus.

In drawing a symbolic parallel between the number seven—the seven rooms of Proust (Combray, Balbec, Paris, Venice, Doncières, summer rooms and winter rooms), Vinteuil's Septet, the deployment of the novel over seven volumes—and Charles Perrault's fairy-tale "Bluebeard," Butor proposes a reading of *In Search* that supports the idea that it can be read as a *noir* novel.[32]

Like Bluebeard, Proust's narrator symbolically kills the women he loves one by one (his grandmother, his mother, the Princess of Guermantes, Gilberte, and Albertine). Furthermore, if Perrault's fairy-tale emphasizes the moral and bourgeois dimension of the story (namely the impossibility of carrying out conjugal duty), Butor's interpretation allows us to bring to the fore the appropriately alchemical aspects of Proust's imagination and their relationship to the idea of the sorcerer's apprentice.[33]

> At Combray, every day, in the late afternoon, long before the moment when I would have to go to bed and stay there, without sleeping, far away from my mother and grandmother, my bedroom again became the fixed and painful focus of my preoccupations. They had indeed hit upon the idea, to distract me on the evenings when they found me looking too unhappy, of giving me a magic lantern, which, while awaiting the dinner hour, they would set on top of my lamp; and, after the fashion of the first architects and master glaziers of the Gothic age, it replaced the opacity of the walls with impalpable iridescences, supernatural multicolored apparitions, where legends were depicted as in a wavering, momentary stain-glassed window.[34]

---

[32] Michel Butor, *Les 7 femmes de Gilbert le mauvais*, in *Arc* (1972), pp. 33-45.
[33] Annick Bouillaguet and Brian G. Rogers, eds., *Dictionnaire Marcel Proust* (Paris: Champion, 2014).
[34] Proust, *Swann's Way*, p. 9.

From the magic lantern of Combray to the impressionist seascapes of the painter Elstir, the Proustian novel develops throughout its narrative the concept of the artist as alchemist who, in his darkened bedroom or his studio, destroys an ancient order to recreate a new one.

> Elstir's studio seemed like the laboratory out of which would come a kind of new creation of the world: from the chaos made of all things we see, he had abstracted, by painting them on various rectangles of canvas now standing about on all sides, glimpses of things, like a wave in the sea crashing its angry lilac-shaded foam down on the sand, or a young man in white twill leaning on a ship's rail. [...]
> As I came in, the creator, paintbrush in hand, was just putting the last touch to the shape of the sun as it set.
> The blinds being down on most sides, the studio was rather cool; and, except for one part where daylight's fleeting decoration dazzled the wall, it was dim; the only window open was a small rectangle framed in honeysuckle, looking out on a strip of garden, then a road; so most of the studio was in half-darkness, transparent and compact in its mass, but moist and glistening at the angles where the light edged it, like a block of rock crystal with one of its sides already cut and polished in patches, so that it shines like a mirror and gives off an iridescent glow. While Elstir, at my request, went on with his painting, I wandered through the chiaroscuro, stopping here and there in front of a picture.[35]

Whether as detective, murderer, sorcerer's apprentice or alchemist, the hero of *In Search* shares a characteristic with the protagonists of film noir: he represents a moment of historical change in the society of which he is a part. In the black and white films of the 1920s, this shift looks ahead to the transition to a modern world of sound and color. For the author and the narrator of *In Search*, the shift represents this same transition to modernity at the turning-point between the sensual indulgence of the Belle

---

[35] Marcel Proust, *In the Shadow of Young Girls in Flower*, trans. James Grieve (New York: Penguin Books, 2002), p. 415.

Epoque[36] and the butchery of World War I. For when that unspeakable and shameful war was over, how would it ever be possible to discover sleep again?

For the author of In Search *a protracted* Voyage to the End of Night *had only just begun.*[37]

---

[36] The Belle Epoque (1871-1914) was a period of high artistic and cultural development in France.
[37] *Voyage to the End of Night* (1932) is a semi-autobiographical novel by Louis-Ferdinand Céline that gives a cynical and nihilistic account of the atrocities of World War I.

Chapter II: Dark Glasses

"I Accuse!"

*The Truth, I want the Truth, for I made a prom-
ise to speak it if justice, when it is referred there,
doesn't speak fully. My duty is to speak out, I do
not wish to be complicit. My nights would be
haunted by the ghost of an innocent man who
dies out there, subject to the most horrifying
torture, for a crime he did not commit.*[38]

Emile Zola

Just before World War I and immediately following the scandal of
the Dreyfus Affair (1894-1906), nothing remained for nineteenth-
century France but to begin singing its first funeral air. It was the
moment to bid goodbye to the old Romantic reverie inherited
from the Revolution. The curtain had just come down on the con-
fident passion of a Positivist faith in the unstoppable progress of
civilization and science. The French Third Republic stepped onto
the stage of the twentieth century and, in a moment of vaudevil-
lian lightness which would come to mark it, Act I began with farce
and falsehood.

In the famous episode from *In the Shadow of Young Girls in Flower*
concerning an afternoon performance at the theatre, young Marcel, curious to see La Berma on stage in the leading role of Racine's
play *Phèdre*, can find little of the poetry of the ancient text in the
many misrepresentations of the modern version. Novelty terrifies
him. His disappointment is complete.

Figure 10, opposite: Formosa Cafe, LA Confidential @2016 fdaubigny

---

[38] "J'Accuse!," is the title of Emile Zola's open letter, published on January 13,
1898 in the newspaper *L'Aurore,* supporting General Dreyfus who had been un-
justly found guilty of high treason by the council of the French Army. Dreyfus,
a general and a Jew, had been accused of betraying war secrets to Germany,
France's enemy. The Dreyfus Affair is a critical moment in the culture of the
French Third Republic because, through a treason trial, it divided the country
into supporters of truth and supporters of falsehood.

This first matinee was, alas, a great disappointment. [...] In one scene, where La Berma stands still for a moment against a backdrop of the sea, with one arm raised to face level, and her whole figure given a greenish tint by an effect of the lighting, the audience had no sooner burst into applause than she changed position and the tableau I wished I could study closely disappeared. I told my grandmother I could not see very well, and she lent me her opera glasses. But when you believe in the reality of things, using an artificial means to see them better is not quite the same as feeling closer to them. I felt it was not La Berma that I was seeing, only an enlarged picture of her. I put the glasses down—but what if the image received by the naked eye was no more accurate, given that it was an image reduced by distance? Which was the true Berma? When she reached Phèdre's declaration of desire for Hippolyte, a part I had been specially looking forward to, because the diction of Oenone and Aricie kept revealing unsuspected subtleties in parts that were not as fine as it, I was sure her intonations would be more striking than any I had contrived to imagine while reading the play at home: but she did not even rise to the effects that the two actresses would have managed; she blurred the whole speech into a toneless recitative, blunting the keen edges of contrasts which any semi-competent performer, even a girl in a school production, could hardly have failed to bring out.[39]

For the young Marcel, modernity rings false; it is heavily made up like an adulterous woman. Truth is not always to be found where one searches for it, not excepting in *In Search*. In Marcel Proust, the question of truth, in art as in life, remains a highly ambivalent (love) affair. While his apprentice novel *Jean Santeuil*, written between 1896 and 1900, is rife with political and social commentary, *In Search of Lost Time*, the novel of his maturity, for its part relegates most of historical discourse to the status of anecdote.

Written in the third person, *Jean Santeuil* employs "he" as a means of relating the opinions of Proust's contemporaries on the truth of the Dreyfus Affair. By transcribing the testimonies of expert

[39] Marcel Proust, *In the Shadow of Young Girls in Flower*, trans. James Grieve (New York: Penguin Viking, 2004), pp. 17, 21.

witnesses in handwriting, law, medicine, and philosophy, the writer carefully takes account of a variety of points of view. Packed with medico-legal commentary, *Jean Santeuil* incorporates the depositions of many witnesses involved in the Affair. For Dr. Laporte, for example, the sentence is obvious: pure science should win out in opposition to the legalistic rhetorical verbiage of generals and judges:

> Any man whose profession it is to seek the truth that lies concealed in handwriting or in the human intestines is in some sort ruthless. The generals, the judges, might be present in all the splendour of uniforms and robes. No matter, he would speak to them of what he knew, and one could feel quite certain that he would not go back on his words because like the doctor who has assumed the role of protector and friend to his patient—a man suffering from congestion of the lungs must not be allowed to go out—he would defend Zola to the best of his ability, and all those others about whom he cared very little but was now going to champion with heat and determination, not because he liked them, but because the handwriting produced by the Court was quite certainly *not* Dreyfus's.[40]

The persistence of scientific language in *Jean Santeuil* invokes the ghostly and archetypal figure of Proust's father, Adrien.[41] It is as though for the young writer the question of truth could only be contemplated in his formative years through scientific objectivity. This mediation, brought about by the *desire for the same* (the father), seems, in fact, to constitute the way forward demanded by an artistic journey—one that will lead the young Marcel Proust to the discovery of his vocation as a writer. In *In Search*, the novel of his maturity, the question of objective truth persists but is inscribed within a much more complex narrative system in which a fictional plot is brought together with scientific discourse. While combining these two discourses, the narrative is mainly built around what is unpredictable. The objectivity of scientific discourse both distorts and consorts with the personal opinions of the narrator, with the result that it is no longer truly possible to be sure whether it is the truth of the law of the novel which dominates

---

[40] Marcel Proust, *Jean Santeuil*, trans. Gerard Hopkins (London: Weidenfeld and Nicolson, 1955), pp. 351-52.
[41] See Chapter 1 and the question of hypnosis.

the story or whether it is the narrator's personal beliefs that sustain it.

figure 11: Dr. Mabuse, *Fritz Lang, 1922*

Noir #3 *Dr. Mabuse*, Fritz Lang (1922)

Marcel Proust died on November 21, 1922. That same year the Austro-Hungarian director Fritz Lang made the silent black and white Expressionist masterpiece, Dr. Mabuse, the Gambler. The first in a short series (The Testament of Dr. Mabuse, 1933), the film was based on the fiction of Luxembourg writer Norbert Jacques, in which the plot hinges on the adventures of the criminal Dr. Mabuse, a specialist in hypnosis and an inveterate gambler. In the 1922 film, the opening scene begins with a surrealistic dialogue between Dr. Mabuse and his factotum, Spoerri. Dr. Mabuse is shuffling a deck of cards which bear the effigy of his next victim. He then thrusts at his servant a hand noticeably trembling from what seems to have been a sleepless night: "You, you have snorted too much cocaine." The criminal is in the midst of creating a plot involving a stock market crash. The second sequence opens on a scene of crooks planning a hold-up of a train that is transporting sacks of banknotes. The viewer, who is also rather dazed, takes part in the mad vision of modernity going at full speed that wants to cannibalize everything in its path. A nascent critic of capitalist society and its speculative financial bubble are sketched in Lang's film and along with them the fakery of the virtual reality they establish. Dr. Mabuse, who abuses[42] as much as possible the weakness and innocence of his victims, makes use of hypnosis to put his patients to sleep and to rob them of their property. He preaches for a revolution in psychoanalysis which would break with the necessity for institutional authority, rupturing and enlarging the circles of truth.

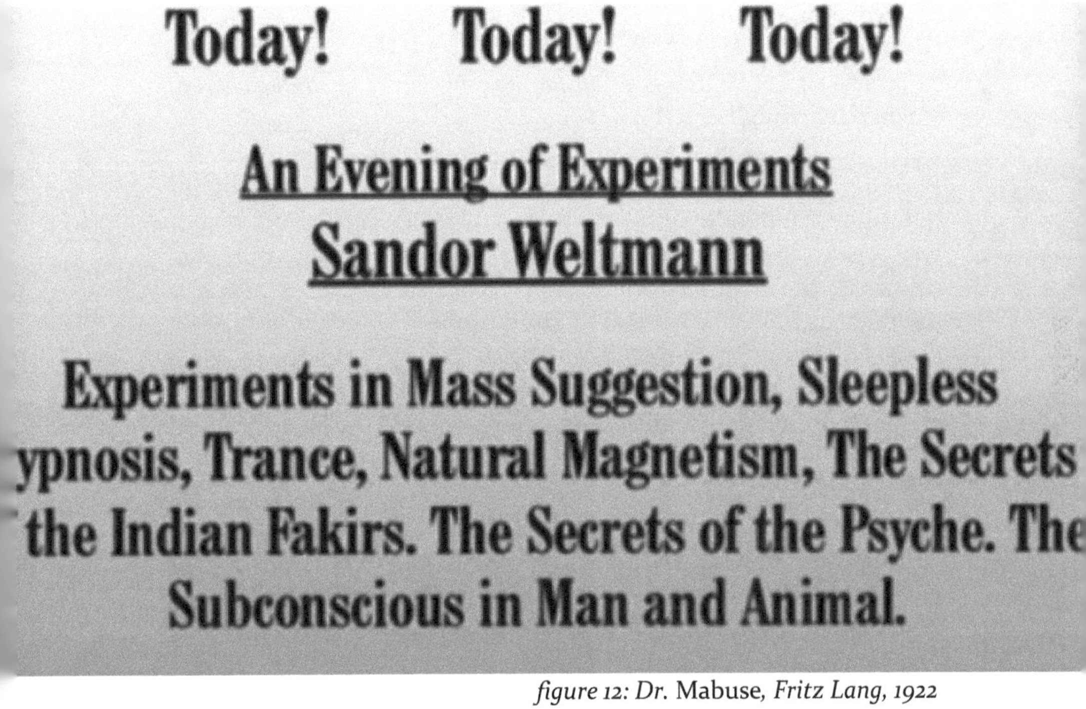

Today!   Today!   Today!

An Evening of Experiments
Sandor Weltmann

Experiments in Mass Suggestion, Sleepless ypnosis, Trance, Natural Magnetism, The Secrets the Indian Fakirs. The Secrets of the Psyche. The Subconscious in Man and Animal.

figure 12: Dr. Mabuse, Fritz Lang, 1922

As in film, the Proustian narrator plays at being Dr. Mabuse. Truth in *In Search of Lost Time* lies always where one least expects it. A little like that inconsequential but fatal woman whom you refuse to notice, that *Woman Next Door*.[43] To add to the diagnosis, the

---

[42] There is a play on words in the original French here between the doctor's name and the verb "abuser," to abuse.

[43] The reference here is to François Truffaut's film *The Woman Next Door* (*La Femme d'à côté*).

narrator of *In Search* also has a grave personality disorder. He splits into two, into more than two. As though the compounding of identities and narrative levels in Proust had the effect of wringing the neck of objective discourse and allowing anarchy in the novelistic game. There are actually three narrators in *In Search*. A young narrator who innocently recounts the days of childhood, an old narrator who recalls, subjectively, scenes from the past, and between those two an omniscient narrator who links them creatively together. An all-knowing intermediary who serves as editor/director, constantly reframing the textual inconsistencies of his two alter egos.

In Search of Lost Time *is all in all nothing but that: a question of cinema, one frame at a time.*

Read the Proustian text as a chronicle announcing the death of intelligence (understood here as objective consciousness) and it becomes easy to understand how the authority of scientific discourse in the hands of the author of *In Search of Lost Time* is periodically undermined and reduced to the simple status of anecdote. Following the great inaugural lesson of *Jean Santeuil*, *In Search* teems with superficial conversations and unimportant exchanges from daily life larded with gossip, idle chat, and unfounded stories.

Even though the Dreyfus Affair was at its height when Proust was writing his monumental novel, the day-to-day events of the war years transposed into the story become a false subject, fake news before its time. That Dreyfus was found guilty of treason is, in fact, relevant for the Verdurin set only to the extent it triggers a game of musical chairs for their mundane social circle—the Duke of Guermantes will be ejected from the chairmanship of the Jockey Club in favour of Mr. Chaussepierre because of his sympathy for General Dreyfus.

The same applies to the tragedy of the British passenger ship, the *Lusitania*, sunk by the Germans in 1915, which in Madame Verdurin's telling is little more than a mere object of gluttony:

> Madame Verdurin, suffering from migraines again now
> that there were no more croissants to dip in her coffee, had

finally obtained an order from Cottard allowing her to have them made for her at a certain restaurant we have spoken about. This had been almost as hard to obtain from the authorities as the appointment of a general. She received the first of these croissants on the morning when the newspapers reported the wreck of the *Lusitania*. As she dipped it in her coffee, and flicked her newspaper with one hand so that it would stay open without her having to remove her other hand from the croissant she was soaking, she said: "How awful! It's worse than the most horrific tragedy." But the loss of all those people at sea must have been a thousand million times reduced before it struck her, because even while she uttered, through a mouthful of croissant, these distressing thoughts, the look which lingered on her face, probably induced by the taste of the croissant, so valuable in preventing migraine, was more like one of quiet satisfaction.[44]

One must know how to traverse the circles of worldly hell in Proust to take the measure of the depth of cynicism of that response. For the soldiers of 1914, the war at the Front and in the trenches was a true hell. In the salons of the Faubourg Saint-Germain, among those who had taken cover far from the Front, it was, with a certain delight, thought about with a cup of tea in hand.

By these clichés and falsifications, the worldly life in Proust somewhat resembles a floating marsh in which the Faubourg's little comedy is engulfed and even sometimes drowned. But when content (truth) disintegrates, style in Proust always comes to the reader's rescue.

The Proustian parenthesis, a recurring narrative device in *In Search*, the linguistic sign of the discursive accident, functions like a life preserver in a story which is often shooting off in all directions.[45] The Proustian parenthesis thus injects the real (truth) when the filaments of the fiction become too light. Just as in film,

---

[44] Marcel Proust, *Finding Time Again*, trans. Ian Patterson (London: Penguin, 2002), pp. 80-81.

[45] Isabelle Serça, "La parenthèse, un 'raccroc' dans le 'bâti' du texte proustien," in *Marcel Proust 3. Nouvelles directions de la recherche proustienne 2.* (Paris-Caen : Lettres Modernes Minard, 2001) : 217-234.

the Proustian parenthesis manages to reset the frame of the image which might otherwise tip into the false and the blurred.

> Each of our actions, our words, our attitudes is cut off from the "world," from the people who have not directly received them, by an ambience whose permeability is infinitely variable and unknown to us; when we learn from experience that some important remark we dearly hoped would be spread about **(like the enthusiastic things I used to say at one time to everyone and at every opportunity about Mme Swann, thinking that among so many scattered seeds at least one would germinate** [my emphasis]) has at once, often because we hoped too hard, been consigned to darkness, then we are hardly likely to start believing that some tiny remark we have forgotten, which we may not even have uttered ourselves but which was formed in the course of events by the imperfect refraction of different words, could be transported, unhindered, infinite distances away—in the present case, to the Princesse de Guermantes—to divert at our expense the banquet of the gods.[46]

There are Rimbaud-like tones of voice similar to *The Drunken Boat* in *In Search of Lost Time*. A desperate attempt to stem the tide of a *Belle Epoque* on the verge of a nervous breakdown and a civilization on the point of shipwreck.[47] Proust's use of the parenthesis is allied to the uncertain geography of an island on which one has landed one morning after a long night of insomnia, a bit by chance; this bit of land which one hangs onto after the night and the gloom of oblivion. As the writer tells us again: "... it is not possible to describe human life without bathing it in the sleep into which it plunges, and which, night after night, encircles it like the sea around a promontory."[48]

---

[46] Marcel Proust, *The Guermantes Way*, trans. Mark Treharne (New York: Penguin Books, 2005), pp. 265-66.

[47] The writer is referring to the method of fishing with a net mentioned in Ruskin's *The Bible of Amiens*, which Proust translated (Paris: Mercure de France, 1947). A note by Proust reads in part: "If you wish to review one of your ideas, even a fleeting example and at a preferred time, you must do so in the spirit of the fishermen: place a net carefully somewhere or other, from one time to another, and it must be constantly renewed." (*Op. cit.*, p. 300.)

[48] Marcel Proust, *The Guermantes Way*, pp. 78-79.

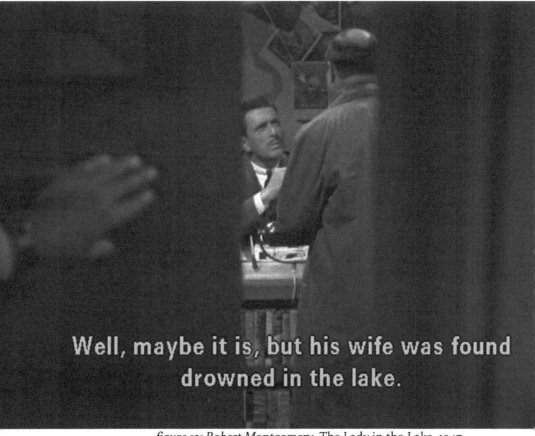

figure 13: Robert Montgomery, The Lady in the Lake, *1947*

NOIR #4 *Lady in the Lake*, Robert Montgomery (1947)

In Montgomery's film noir, inspired by Steve Fisher's screenplay and adapted from Raymond Chandler's novel, we find the legendary private detective Philip Marlowe. Hired by Adrienne Fromsett, the director of a Los Angeles public relations firm to look into the disappearance of Krystal Kingsby, the wife of an ultra-rich publisher, the detective leads the search. Soon enough the body of a woman is dredged from Little Fawn Lake several hours from Los Angeles. The victim might well be the wife of Kingsby himself. The investigation continues and the situation gets more complicated. The story is told entirely from a subjective point of view with a hand-held camera— in the Hollywood of the time, a cutting-edge technical accomplishment. In this open-frame story the viewer is invited to participate in solving the puzzle of the murder. Just as in the Proustian novel, the telling of the story works on several narrative levels. The subjective narration of the detective, the hand-held camera, the objective narration (of the omniscient narrator) when, for only a few seconds in the film, Marlowe appears opposite a mirror in front of the camera and, between the two, the viewer's own interpretation.[49] Montgomery's film enjoyed great success at the box office, as much due to its originality as to the brisk publicity campaign led by MGM, which covered the walls of Los Angeles with posters: "YOU and Robert Montgomery solve a murder mystery together." "YOU accept an invitation to the blonde's apartment."

---

[49] It should be pointed out that the given name "Marcel" is explicitly used only twice in *In Search.*

figure 14: Robert Montgomery, The Lady in the Lake, *1947*

Truth is not always where you think it will be found. It is often hidden in the apartment of the woman next door.[50] *Except that, for Truffaut, the blonde was a brunette.*

Truth in Proust, hidden likewise at the bottom of the lake, always eventually emerges, but it remains fragmentary, partial, even incomplete.[51] To be imagined even partially, it requires the same active involvement of the reader as a Montgomery film.

---

[50] See note 6.
[51] Yves Tadié, *Le Lac Inconnu : Entre Proust et Freud* (Paris: Gallimard, 2012).

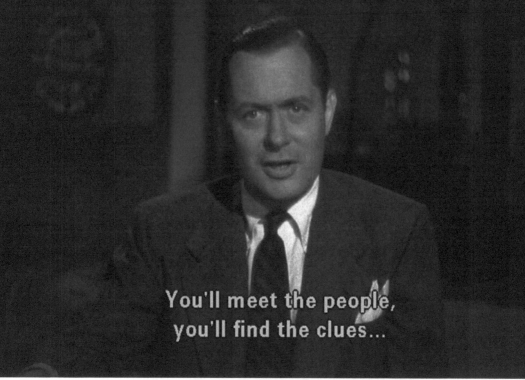

figure 15: Robert Montgomery, The Lady in the Lake, *1947*

Thus with Proust there is no final moment of transfiguration as there is in the poetry of Dante, but rather a chiaroscuro of consciousness that leaves truth in the work suspended, and with it a taste for a kind of mystery. Isn't the mystery of the little patch of yellow wall in *In Search* the fundamental enigma which obsesses the writer Bergotte for his entire life, and perhaps Proust himself too? The writer Bergotte, surely a stand-in for the author, dies of a stroke as he stands before a Vermeer painting and realizes only too late the profound barrenness of his own style:

> [...] he fixed his gaze, as a child does on a yellow butterfly he wants to catch, on the precious little patch of wall. 'That is how I should have written,' he said to himself. My last books are too dry, I should have applied several layers of colour, made my sentences precious in themselves, like that little patch of yellow wall.' He knew how serious his dizziness was. In the heavenly scales he could see,

weighing down one of the pans, his own life, while the other contained the little patch of wall so beautifully painted in yellow. He could feel that he had rashly given the first for the second. 'I would really rather not, he thought, be the human interest item in this exhibition for the evening papers.' He was repeating to himself, 'Little patch of yellow wall with a canopy, little patch of yellow wall.' While saying this he collapsed on to a circular sofa; then suddenly he stopped thinking that his life was in danger and said to himself, 'It's just indigestion, those potatoes were undercooked.' He had a further stroke, rolled off the sofa on to the ground as all the visitors and guards came running up. He was dead. Dead forever? Who can say?[52]

Patches and plans. A question of cinema, one frame at a time.

Given the especially elusive nature of truth in Proust, the method chosen for interpreting the novel (and this essay) can only be inquisitorial. Like in a police investigation. Suspicion in Proust is never-ending, as it were, and a trial is always about to take place. Given this, textual criticism of Proust is not off the mark. In light of the proliferation of preliminary texts, the extensive sketches and notebooks left behind by the author, all of which render the work an indecipherable mass of signs and clues, the reader must confront a single requirement: to follow the author (the guilty party) on the trail better to confuse him.

For example, consider the passage concerning "the little room smelling of orris root." If the final version in *Swann's Way* is less explicit than in the sketches that preceded it, sketches that were published after the author's death in 1922,[53] only a textual study, which might be compared to a forensic study (after all, we speak of digging up texts), allows us to be specific about the small ways in which the author camouflages the truth.[54]

---

[52] Marcel Proust, *The Prisoner*, trans. Carol Clark (London: Penguin Books, 2002), pp. 169-70.
[53] Marcel Proust, *Jean Santeuil* (Paris : Gallimard, 1952 ; English trans. 1955) and *Contre Sainte-Beuve* (Paris : Gallimard, 1954).
[54] See the detailed textual analysis of Than-Vân Ton-That, "Enjeux et méthodes de l'interprétation chez Proust : censures et métamorphoses du 'petit cabinet

In Proust, the foulness of the crime is increased twofold, as it were, by his efforts to bury it. Is the narrator like a burrowing wasp?[55] The practices of censorship and self-censorship are certainly well-known writerly strategies, above all when it is a question of concealing unorthodox sexual behaviour.

In an effort to understand a little more clearly this other *affair*, let us try to compare several distinct versions of the drama available to us for study. For the purposes of our inquiry, let us set side by side three episodes of the same *crime*, which through their similarities and differences will perhaps tell us something about the identity of their author.

Episode no. 1 from *Jean Santeuil*: "What caught his attention was **a humble caterpillar** with a brown velvet coat embroidered with green silk seeming like an omen at the foot of a hot and beautifully sunny wall which it was attempting to climb. [...] With a heart made joyful by this irrefutable sign of the presence of the God of Summer, he went on watching it with sympathy, without threatening **a sacrilegious hand** against this favorite of God, much more his child, born of him perhaps even that morning, who set out at once on **his task of leaving a silver trail to mark** his passage over the earth, silently, no sooner arrived than it started over, facing setbacks with aplomb, continuing to follow its path like a creature owed **a day full of glory**, a creature promised the infinite extent of heaven. [...] **This little room was on an upstairs floor**. [...] He had just discovered in himself the marvelous essence of a pleasure as new, **as ravishing, as dissimilar from the everyday pleasures of the world as the lilac or the gloomy iris**, a pleasure that the hot sun seemed to magnify, and which seemed

---

sentant l'iris'," *La Lecture littéraire, Université de Reims*, no. 1 (November 1996) : 41-58.

[55] "And like the hymenopteran observed by Fabre, the burrowing wasp who, so that its young may have fresh meat to eat after its death, summons anatomy in aid of its cruelty and, after capturing a few weevils and spiders, proceeds with a marvelous knowledge and skill to pierce them in the nerve center that governs the movements of their legs but not their other life functions, in such a way that the paralyzed insect near which it deposits its eggs provides the larvae, when they hatch, with prey that is docile, harmless, incapable of flight or resistance, but not in the least tainted..." Marcel Proust, *Swann's Way*, trans. Lydia Davis, p. 126.

to give to life some eternally soft character that until then it had lacked [...]"[56]

Episode no. 2 from *Against Sainte-Beuve*: "It was an unusually spacious room for a water-closet. The door locked securely, but the window always stood open, to accommodate a young lilac which having taken root in the outside wall had pushed its scented head through the aperture. [...] **Then, in search of a pleasure that I did not know, I began to explore myself**, and if I had been engaged in performing **a surgical operation on my brain** and marrow I could not have been more agitated, more terrified. [...] In that moment I felt a sort of **caress** surrounding me. It was the scent of lilac-blossom, which in my excitement I had grown unaware of. **But a bitter smell, like the smell of sap, was mixed with it, as though I had snapped the branch. I had left a trail on the leaf, silvery and natural as a thread of gossamer or a snail-track,** that was all. But on that bough, it seemed to me like the forbidden fruit on the Tree of Knowledge; and like the races that give non-human form to their deities, for some time afterward it was in the guise of this almost interminably extensible silvery thread which I had to spin out of myself by going widdershins to the normal course of my life that I pictured **the devil**.[57]

Episode no. 3 from *In Search of Lost Time*: "I went up **to sob** at the very top of the house next to the schoolroom, under the roofs, **in a little room that smelled of orris root** and was also perfumed by a wild black-currant bush which had sprouted outside between the stones of **the wall** and extended a branch of flowers through the half-open window. Intended for a **more specialized** and **more vulgar** use, this room, from which during the day you could see all the way to the keep of Roussainville-le-Pin, for a long time served me as a refuge, no doubt because it was the only one I was permitted to lock, for all those occupations of mine that demanded an inviolable **solitude: reading, reverie, tears**, and **sensuous pleasure**." (Phrases in bold are my emphases.)[58]

---

[56] Marcel Proust, *Jean Santeuil* (Paris: Gallimard, 1971), p. 294. (Translated by BW).
[57] Marcel Proust, *By Way of Sainte-Beuve*, trans. Sylvia Townsend Warner (London: Chatto & Windus, 1958), pp. 24-25.
[58] Marcel Proust, *Swann's Way*, trans. Lydia Davis, pp. 12-13.

In the first extract from the youthful novel *Jean Santeuil,* written between 1896 and 1900 and first published in 1952, the narrator finds himself outside in a natural setting. The little room, like an allegory of social conventions, is located "a floor above." Alone, free, and dedicated to exploring his inner life, the young man places a sacrilegious hand on a "humble" chenille bedspread, which in return releases a "fine silver thread," the promise of un-known, glorious, and eternal pleasures.

In the second extract from *Contre Sainte-Beuve,* written between 1895 and 1900 and first published in 1954, Proust, as always, alle-gorizes the sexual act, but this time lends it a religious connotation with a hint of sacrilege. The youthful tenderness associated with innocence in the earlier excerpt gives way to a process of rational-izing the act of masturbation. The effort of making conscious and of moralization little by little works to vitiate the meaning of the innocent gesture in the 1952 episode, with the result that the for-bidden pleasure here assumes a bitter taste and diffuses an "acrid smell."

Finally, in the third excerpt, taken from *Swann's Way,* the first vol-ume of *In Search of Lost Time,* the scalpel of analysis makes a deeper cut and, in the end, almost nothing remains of the scene of the *crime.* The body is entirely emptied of its "substantific marrow" (to use Rabelais's term), of its organs, of its viscera, and all that remains on the table is a mass of concepts, generalizations, and proper names (literally as well as figuratively): "refuge, solitude, reading, and tears."
The act of burrowing is thus total. The object of the crime has en-tirely disappeared. For the reader, all that remains is an operator's manual, a list of instructions. The narrator's feeling of guilt gives way to a feeling of imprisonment. The young man is now shut up under the eaves in the little room which smells of orris, near the wall, weeping.

Who holds him prisoner? His mother, surely. According to the fi-nal reports of the inquiry, it can be said that the dates coincide almost exactly. Proust's mother, Jeanne Proust-Weil, died on Sep-tember 26, 1905. It is highly likely that Proust, out of the deep affection and tenderness he felt for his mother, so as not to hurt her feelings and to disguise his sexual practices, preferred to allegorize the scene by reducing it to a religious and mythological fable.

For Marcel, it was almost a perfect crime.

figure 16: Billy Wilder, Double Indemnity, *1944*

CHAPTER III. BLACK MAGIC

She is like the heart of a flower without heart.

André Breton, *Nadja*

To my only desire. High-born and proud, a woman stands straight. She seems to hold in a circle around her the sequence of the hours of the day, the order of time and years.[59] Close by her can be found a young woman and several companion animals. The whiteness of her complexion and the narrowness and length of her face contrast with the roundness of a blue island, divided by a blue tent, and surrounded by a red background. She is carefully depositing a pearl necklace in a jewel-box held out to her. Across the top of the tent in which she has taken shelter is written—mysteriously, in gold letters—the motto "TO MY ONLY DESIRE."

Our inquiry begins anew.

While many interpretations of it exist with no definitive resolution, the enigma of the sixth panel of the *Lady and the Unicorn* tapestries, an anonymous masterpiece from the French Middle Ages, which can be admired today at the Musée de Cluny in Paris,[60] continues to provoke the viewer. Before that viewer, as in a film, unfurl one by one the scenes of a drama that, while ancient, possesses modern overtones, a drama that would have a femme fatale as its central protagonist, not yet given that name, but already embodying the *gesta*.[61]

Figure 17, opposite: Kiss me deadly, West of Los Angeles @2016 fdaubigny

---

[59] This is a reference to the opening pages of *In Search of Lost Time*: "A sleeping man holds in a circle around him the sequence of the hours, the order of the years and worlds." See Chapter 1, note 1.

[60] The Musée de Cluny is formally known as the Musée nationale du Moyen-Âge.

[61] Jean-Patrice Boudet, "La Dame à la licorne et ses sources médiévales d'inspiration," *Bulletin de la Société nationale des antiquaires de France*, Meeting of February 10, 1999, pp. 61-78.

figure 18: Dame à la Licorne, *Musée de Cluny, Paris, France*

To my only desire. Historians have not been mistaken in considering it an error to long for a singular meaning in Tapestry no. 6. In the case of the *Lady and the Unicorn*, is the desire that of the lover who holds his lady captive, or is it that of a proud woman celebrating the early victories of her *femen* independence? Does the motto "To my only desire" echo the fieriness of a passionate heart, or the sincerity of a vow of chastity taken in order to tamp down the ardor of an overwhelming passion?[62]

---

[62] At the end of the Middle Ages and in the sixteenth century, the French verb "désirer" could be synonymous with "apaiser" (calm, soothe, tamp down) or "regretter" (regret, feel sorry, miss), particularly in the context of contrition linked to the disappearance of the loved one. See Frédéric Godefroy, *Dictionnaire de l'ancienne langue française et de tous ses dialectes du XIe au XVe siècle* (Paris: 1883; Nendeln: Kraus Reprint,1969), II: 600; Frédéric Godefroy, *Dictionnaire de l'ancien français* (Paris: 1990), p. 134; Edmond Huguet, *Dictionnaire de la langue*

However the circle is to be squared, the mystery remains and with it the image of a woman pulled in two directions, right in the middle of a conflict which will form part of the western imagination: the sacred and profane marriage of love and death. *Mors* and *Amor. Eros* and *Thanatos. The virgin and the whore.*

> A,[63] the black velvet cuirass of flies whose essence
> commingles, abuzz, around the cruellest of smells,
> Wells of shadow;[64]

The vowel A, like the black cuirass of the black widow, chants Rimbaud's verb. Before him was the song of troubadour poet Alain Chartier, also a prisoner of the Beautiful Woman and his desire:

> Not long agoo, ryding an esy paas,
> I felle in thought, of joy ful desperate
> With gret disease and payn, so that I was
> Of al lovers the moost unfortunate,
> Sith by hire dart moost cruell, ful of hate,
> The deth hath take my lady and maistres
> And left me soul, thus discomfit and mate,
> Sore languishing and in wey of distress.[65]

In the poem "La Belle dame sans mercy" (1424), composed in the same period as the *Lady and the Unicorn* tapestry, the *Belle Dame* already appears in the guise of a dangerous Circe character who puts her victims' reason to sleep and bewitches unto death anyone who looks on her. The *femme fatale*, before the term existed in common usage, is a Scheherazade who likes to spend time in bed with her victims but prefers never to fall asleep. *In the Proustian fashion.*

---

française au XVIe siècle (Paris: Champion, 1946), III: 85. This meaning corresponds also to one of the meanings of *desiderium* in classical Latin.

[63] The capital letter A in Rimbaud's poem is the first letter of the French word for love (*amour*), a fact that is lost in the English translation. The capital letter A is also the initial letter of the word inscribed on the tent in the sixth panel of the Lady and the Unicorn tapestry.

[64] Arthur Rimbaud, "Vowels," translated by Christian Bök (Wagsrevue.com/download/issue_3/voyelles.pdf).

[65] Alain Chartier, "La Belle dame sans mercy," ll. 29-36, trans. Richard Roos and first printed in English in 1526.

In any case, it was not only [Vinteuil's] music that Albertine played for me; the pianola sometimes served us as a kind of educational (historical and geographical) magic lantern, and on the walls of that room in Paris, better equipped than the old one in Combray, I saw spread out, according as Albertine played some Rameau or some Borodin, now an eighteenth-century tapestry dotted with cherubs on a background of roses, and now the Eastern steppes where sounds are lost in the limitless distances and muffled by the snow. And these fleeting decorations were in fact the only ones in my room, for, even though when I came into my inheritance from Aunt Léonie I had promised myself I would be a collector like Swann, buying pictures and statues, in fact all my money went on horses, a motor-car, dresses for Albertine. But then, did not my room contain a work of art more precious than all those others? It was Albertine herself.[66]

If the prose of Proust, the romantic poetry of Rimbaud or that of Keats in the nineteenth century, take up the same motif of the "Belle Dame Sans Mercy,"[67] the theme itself is also used in American film noir of the 1940s.[68]

NOIR #5 *The Big Sleep*, Howard Hawks (1946)

Philip Marlowe. Profession, detective. Raymond Chandler's invention is like a modern knight in a linen suit who frequents the shadier corners of Los Angeles, the haunts of bums, aging crazy men and dangerous women. In his search for truth, he chases after dragons and knocks out a few of their teeth, while also, tragically, falling in love with fairies. Howard Hawks's full-length feature, *The Big Sleep* (1946), adapted from a screenplay by Chandler, winks almost imperceptibly at the characters of the medieval legend of the Belle Dame. In *The Big Sleep*, Vivian Sternwood (Lauren Bacall) recreates the figure of the Lady of the Lake, the enchantress Vivian.

---

[66] Marcel Proust, *The Prisoner*, trans. Carol Clark (London: Penguin Books, 2002), p. 353.
[67] John Keats, "La Belle Dame Sans Merci," in *John Keats*, ed. Elizabeth Cook (Oxford and New York: Oxford University Press, 1994), pp. 166-67.
[68] In 1920 Germaine Dulac directed a film entitled *La Belle Dame Sans Merci*.

figure 19: Howard Hawks, The Big Sleep, *1946*

Like the fairy in the Arthurian legend, the femme fatale, appearing suddenly and out of the blue, seduces while she destroys by lulling her victims' better judgement.[69] According to the pattern set by La Belle Dame Sans Mercy, the femme fatale has only one desire: an overwhelming impulse to mix blood, life and death. Tattooed with scandal's scarlet (i.e. purplish black) letter, often as obscure in her origins as she is in her motivations, she is a perfect enigma: which is to say, unsolvable.

---

[69] Mary Wertheim, "Philip Marlowe: Knight in Blue Serge," *Columbia Library Columns* 37, 2 (1988), pp. 13-22.

A figurehead in American film noir during the 1940s, the *femme fatale* holds out a personal mirror to her victim and to society and, in the uncertainty of her game, reflects the personal or social conflicts of the culture for which she represents pure fantasy.

> Brigid (The Maltese Falcon) is the archetypal hardboiled heroine: beautiful, apparently helpless and victimized, drawing the detective into the intrigue and then exploiting his particular talents—and his naive romanticism— in her perverse quest for wealth and power. Spade, after he has become Brigid's, realizes that he is simply another of her victims, and none of her entreaties is effective at the end of the film.[70]

The femme fatale as a metaphor for the beautiful Dame who lulls her victims to sleep often goes together with the allegorization of her as a "flower of evil." Yet that process is already classic given its common appearance in European literature since the nineteenth century. Théophile Gautier, for example, in his novel *Captain Fracasse*, draws a distinction between "the common flowers of a modest charm" and "the exotic flowers in outlandish forms" associated with arrogance and the seven deadly sins.

> [...] besides which these plants that take bizarre forms, in strange colors, with rare scents, and did not have the modest attractiveness of ordinary flowers; their self-conscious beauty recalled that of Vallembreuse [in the Gautier novel] and was too similar to him.[71]

The exotic bloom, characteristically an orchid, becomes a "taciturn" flower in Huysmans' *Against the Grain*, while in Maupassant it is imagined as "a strange girl." In Zola, the tropical flower is often compared to a "bizarre" plant, which, by its oddness of form and shape, presents us with the weakness of a failed species.[72]

---

[70] James M. Maxfield, "La Belle Dame Sans Merci and the Neurotic Knight: Characterization in *The Maltese Falcon*," in his *The Fatal Woman: Sources of Male Anxiety in American Film Noir 1941-1991* (Madison, NJ: Farleigh Dickinson University Press, 1996), p. 16.

[71] From Gautier's *Captain Fracasse*, quoted in Régine Boerderie, *Bizarre, bizarrerie: De Constant à Proust* (Grenoble: ELLUG, 2011), pp. 184-87.

[72] Ibid.

Then, a border of begonias and Caladium surrounded the plantings of trees; [...] bizarre plants whose foliage lives a strange life with a sombre or washed-out burst of sickly blossoms. [...] And under the vaults, between the beds of trees, here and there, small iron chains outline flower beds in which orchids were ranged, bizarre plants hanging in mid-air, which thrust from everywhere their fat shoots, gnarled and lopsided like twisted limbs.[73]

NOIR #6, *The Big Sleep*, Howard Hawks (continued)

In Howard Hawks's film, the same infirmity strikes General Sternwood (Charles Waldron). Disabled by wounds he suffered during the war, when he commanded a military brigade in the Irish Republican Army, the General subsequently devotes his time to the only thing permitted him by his grand old age and his insomnia: the cultivation of orchids. The first minutes of the film allow the viewer to enter the cloistered world of the General. Here we find Marlowe, the detective in a linen suit, who has come to investigate the motives of an earlier crime. The first scene of the film gives us the General's youngest daughter, Carmen Sternwood, who, as a welcoming gesture, does a lubricious dance around a large potted rose bush. However, the detective will show that he is untouched by the young Lolita's provocative moves, and the scene ends on a first vegetal metaphor: "You ought to wean her. She is old enough," says Marlowe to the porter. In the next scene, this time Marlowe enters the General's tropical greenhouse. The old man shares with the detective his love of orchids—which he indulges by proxy but also to a fault.

---

[73] Quoted from Zola's novel *La Curée* (*The Kill*) in ibid.

General: Do you like orchids?
Marlowe: Not particularly.
General: Ugh. Nasty things. Their flesh is too much like the flesh of men, and their perfume has the rotten sweetness of corruption.

-Do you like orchids?
-Not particularly.

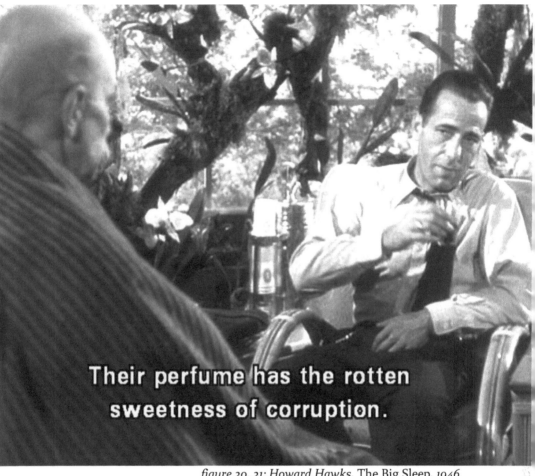

Their perfume has the rotten
sweetness of corruption.

figure 20, 21: Howard Hawks, The Big Sleep, *1946*

In the third scene, we see Marlowe sweating profusely, like a poisonous tropical plant. The sleuth then enters the bedroom, where he finds the General's second daughter, Mrs. Vivian Sternwood (Lauren Bacall). The scene of their meeting initiates the circles of hell. Alone in the room, Marlowe is on edge. He feels that danger is immanent. Lost in the shadows in a corner of the room stands Vivian, proud and self-assured. Like a femme fatale before the murder, she holds a glass in her hand.

figure 22: Howard Hawks, The Big Sleep, *1946*

To my only desire. In Proust, the *femme fatale* also embodies a flower of evil. Moreover, the writer's sexual botany is created especially in her image. The narrator of *In Search* suggests a scale going from "true flowers" and "worldly flowers" to "captive" and "precious" flowers.

> Whether it is that the faith which creates has dried up in me, or that reality takes shape in memory alone, the flowers I am shown today for the first time do not seem to me to be real flowers. The Méséglise way with its lilacs, its hawthorns, its cornflowers, its poppies, its apple trees, the Guermantes way with its river full of tadpoles, its

water lilies and buttercups, formed for me for all time the contours of the countryside where I would like to live, where I demand above all else that I may go fishing, drift about in a boat, see ruins of Gothic fortifications, and find among the wheat fields a church, like Saint-André-des-Champs, monumental, rustic, and golden as a haystack; and the cornflowers, the hawthorns, the apple trees that I still happen, when traveling, to come upon in the fields, because they are situated at the same depth, on the level of my past, communicate immediately with my heart.[74]

If the innocence of childhood is reflected in a botany of characteristics that are "naive and rustic," such as are found in wild roses, or hawthorns, everything else is the poetry of orchids which, in Proust, as in Howard Hawks's movie, represent the corruption of manners, in the city and the society as a whole. Associated with love for sale, with bisexuality and homosexuality, orchids bring back to life the *topos* of the flower of evil from classical literature. "To make cattleya" being Odette's code word when she wants to indicate to her lover her wish to make love, the orchid is thus the flower that, in Proust, ultimately symbolizes the display, disguise, and deceptiveness of the world of prostitutes and sexual inverts.

The door of the shop closed on them, and I could no longer hear anything. I had lost sight of the bumblebee, I did not know whether it was the insect that the orchid needed, but I no longer doubted the miraculous possibility of a very rare insect and a captive flower being conjoined, now that M. de Charlus (a simple comparison of the providential chances, whatever they might be, without the least scientific pretension to drawing a parallel between certain botanical laws and what is sometimes quite wrongly called homosexuality) who for years past had come into this house only at the times when Jupien was not there, had, through the accident of Mme de Villeparisis's indisposition, encountered the waistcoat maker and, with him, the good fortune reserved for men of the Baron's kind by one of those fellow creatures who may even be, as we shall see, infinitely younger than Jupien and better-looking, the man predestined so that they may receive their share of sensual

---

[74] Marcel Proust, *Swann's Way*, trans. Lydia Davis, pp. 188-89.

pleasure on this earth: the man who loves only elderly gentlemen.[75]

The conjoining of the laws of botany and of homosexuality are not in any case the expression of a simple fantasy (or evasion) on the part of the writer, but form the object of a deep and well documented element of research.[76] If the expression "to make cattleya" is derived from the name of the English botanist and horticulturalist William Cattley (1788-1835), who in the nineteenth century discovered a new variety of orchid native to Brazil, the homosexual connection in *In Search* between the bumblebee and the orchid arises more generally from scientific discoveries made at the beginning of the twentieth century concerning the laws of plant reproduction and, more particularly, to observations made by Darwin.[77]

Following Darwin it is now known that orchids are in fact hermaphroditic plants, i.e. they possess both male and female sexual organs but require fertilization by insects, because the pollen produced in the stamen cannot make contact on its own with the pistil, the female organ.

As a flower ripe for chance sexual union, the Proustian orchid is thus the very model of the scandalous plant. And in Proust, scandal is always declared by a woman—and if by a man, he is still a woman! "M. de Charlus had the look of a woman. He was one!," cries the narrator.[78]

Moreover for Proust, the flowers of evil bear a nimbus of exotic scents. Traditionally associated with an Orient to be found only in literature, they often evoke regions of distant lands. Whether under the name Dido (Virgil), Cleopatra (William Shakespeare), *Madame Chrysanthemum* (Pierre Loti), Salomé (Gustave

---

[75] Marcel Proust, *Sodom and Gomorrah*, trans. John Sturrock (New York: Penguin Books, 2004), pp. 8-9.

[76] Proust's knowledge of flowers is usually attributed to his reading of works such as Gaston Bonnier's *La Flore* or Maeterlinck's *L'Intelligence des fleurs*. See Annick Bouillaguet and Brian G. Rogers, eds., *Dictionnaire Marcel Proust* (Paris: Champion, 2004), p. 386.

[77] Charles Darwin, *Fertilization of Orchids* (London: John Murray, 1862).

[78] Marcel Proust, *Sodom and Gomorrah*, trans. John Sturrock, p. 16.

Flaubert), or *Madama Butterfly* (Giacomo Puccini), the *femme fatale* always comes from a foreign country, where the faculties of reason and judgement are in abeyance.

In Proust's novel Albertine, the ideal *femme fatale*, is thus associated with dreams of Venice, the Oriental city. If the East is a poetic motif that keeps surfacing in *In Search*, from the Gothic architecture of the church at Balbec[79] to the slivers of moon lighting up a Paris transformed during the war into a Bosphorus-like landscape, the author will devote almost a whole volume (*The Prisoner/The Fugitive*) to the steamy poetry of Venice, a city on which the image of his passionate but long-dead love affairs is printed in relief.

Venice, the city of water, fleeting and unknowable, carved in Albertine's image, immerses the narrator then in an epistemological difficulty where every effort at rational explanation fails.

> Female sexuality is spread out over the body, signified by all of its parts. And it is the very non-localizability of this sexuality that defines her as a proper "other" to the man whose sex is *in place*, a reassurance of mastery and control. Woman thus becomes the other side of knowledge as it is conceived within the phallocentric logic. She is epistemological trouble.[80]

If the *femme fatale* is irreducibly *The Woman Next Door*,[81] fundamentally *other*, then the weird and watery uniqueness of Venice becomes the natural element in the Proustian novel, symbiotic and symbolic. Venice is no longer that island familiar to cartographers and located to the south of Italy; it becomes the narrator's private and intimate Map of Love.

> [She] had always hidden [it] from me, keeping me away from it, as a woman might have hidden from me the fact that she was an enemy spy, yet more treacherously than such a spy, who deceives only regarding her nationality, whereas Albertine deceived me regarding the nature of

---

[79] Proust's fictional town is named after Baalbek in Lebanon.
[80] Mary Ann Doane, *Femmes Fatales: Feminism, Film Theory, Psychoanalysis* (New York: Routledge, 2016), pp. 102-03.
[81] François Truffaut, *La Femme d'à côté* (1981).

> her deepest being, in that she did not belong to the com-
> mon race of humanity, but to an alien breed that
> intermingles with it and hides within it, but never en-
> tirely fuses with it.[82]

Faithful to her desire and to her secret, the *femme fatale* remains ever a mystery. Anyone who investigates her becomes her prisoner. The aspirant captor is always himself captured. When the detective and the *femme fatale* come face to face, their initial gaze unavoidably starts up the hellish mechanics of desire. A moment of enchantment. A moment frozen in time.

> What is that time of arrest of the movement? It is simply
> the fascinatory effect, in that it is a question of dispos-
> sessing the evil eye of the gaze, in order to ward it off.

> The evil eye is the *fascinum*, it is that which has the effect
> of arresting movement and, literally, of killing life. At the
> moment the subject stops, suspending his gesture, he is
> mortified. [83]

When the Belle Dame becomes a Gorgon, she is licensed to kill.[84]

---

[82] Marcel Proust, *The Fugitive*, trans. Peter Collier (London: Penguin Books, 2002), p. 493.

[83] Jacques Lacan, *The Seminar of Jacques Lacan*, ed. Jacques-Alain Miller, Book XI: *The Four Fundamental Concepts of Psychoanalysis*, trans. Alan Sheridan (New York and London: W.W. Norton, 1998), p. 118.

[84] In Greek mythology, the Gorgon or Medusa was a goddess whose gaze had the power of turning anyone who looked at her to stone.

The machinery had
started to move
and nothing could stop it.

figure 23, 24: Billy Wilder, Double Indemnity, *1944*

NOIR #7 *Double Indemnity*, Billy Wilder (1944)

Shifted into cinema, the moment of fascination becomes Billy Wilder's long camera take focusing on the bejewelled ankle of Phyllis (Barbara Stanwyck) walking downstairs. By reimagining the poetic theme of Duchamp's Nude Descending a Staircase, the even, measured, and self-confidant movement of the low-born and proud Phyllis mimics the hellish mechanics of desire in which the insurance man, Neff (Fred MacMurray), will find himself crushed.[85] This masterpiece of American film noir shot in the 40s on the east side of Los Angeles dramatizes once again a Belle Dame Sans Mercy who, to avoid the clutches of her rich husband, will take advantage of the insurance salesman's naiveté to plan a crime disguised as an accidental death in order the get life insurance money, power, and freedom.

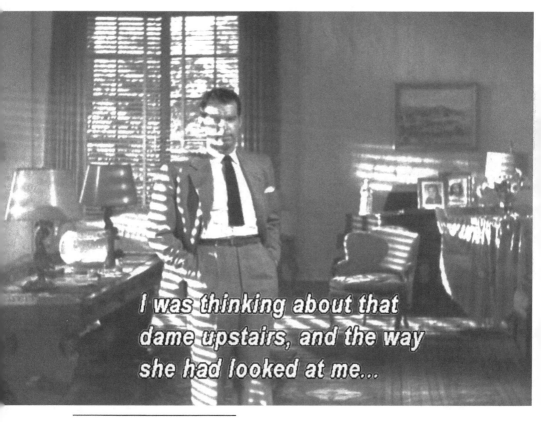

I was thinking about that dame upstairs, and the way she had looked at me...

---

[85] Marcel Duchamp, *Nue descendant un escalier* [Nude Descending a Staircase], 1912.

and I wanted
to see her again, close...

figure 25, 26: Billy Wilder, Double Indemnity, *1944*

This same taste for long takes that glorify the desired woman can be found in Proust's *In Search*. In particular, long takes on Albertine's face surprised during sleep. Almost uniformly in Proust sleep is understood as this counter-fascinatory moment of arrested movement that might at last allow the character to be *taken in*, to penetrate her secret and to hold on to its truth.

In that way her sleep realized, to a certain degree, the promise of love; [...] When she was asleep, I did not have to speak any more, I knew that she could not see me, I did not have to live on the surface of myself. By closing her eyes, by losing consciousness, Albertine had put off, one by one, the various marks of humanity which had so disappointed me in her, from the day that we first met. She was animated only by the unconscious life of plants, of trees, a life more different from my own, stranger, and yet which I possessed more securely. Her individuality did not break through at every moment, as it did when we talked, through unconfessed thoughts and unguarded looks. She had drawn back into herself all the parts of her that were normally on the outside, she had taken refuge, enclosed and summed up in her body. Watching her, watching her in my hands, I felt that I possessed her completely, in a way I never did when she was awake.[86]

In Proust, however, the possibility of love, i.e. the moment of truth, lasts only briefly: the time of sleep, something that in Proustian terms means an impossible or at least always unstable time. Between wakefulness and sleep, truth like love in Proust can only be experienced intermittently.[87] In the face of the impossibility of love and truth, only two possibilities remain for the quester: accept the mystery or force the truth and die. The *femme fatale* always resists, that is her deepest instinct. By definition she is utterly closed to the hermeneutic code. Both the detective and the narrator of *In Search* will attempt to penetrate the mystery in vain. Any attempt is doomed to failure.

---

[86] Marcel Proust, *The Prisoner*, trans. Carol Clark, p. 60.
[87] The original title of Proust's novel was *The Intermittences of the Heart*, but by 1913 he would finally settle on *In Search of Lost Time*.

And I still think that you're hiding something.

figure 27: Roman Polanski, Chinatown, *1974*

Color # 1 *Chinatown*, Roman Polanski (1974)

In this film noir by Roman Polanski shot in Los Angeles, in which the plot hinges on the real-life scandal of water diversion from the Owens Valley, the search for truth is almost always checked by failure. The detective Gittes (Jack Nicholson) comes to realize too late that the temptress Evelyn Mulwray (Faye Dunaway) is at once both guilty and the victim of the story which he is investigating.[88] Between his own misunderstandings and the impossibility of interpreting the clues, the sleuth's clumsiness will not only result in the death of Evelyn, the woman he loves, but also in leaving untouched a corrupt political system. For Gittes, nothing remains save a single outcome between living and dying: oblivion. And so the final line of the film, after the detective has lost everything: "Forget it, Jake. It's Chinatown."

---

[88] Evelyn is the victim of incest by her father, who is none other than the partner of the chief engineer on the construction of the Los Angeles viaduct that will divert water from the Owens Valley. This project will be at the heart of one of the greatest corruption stories of the century.

Forget it, Jake.
It's Chinatown.

figure 28: Roman Polanski, Chinatown, *1974*

At the end of *The Fugitive*, after the disappearance and death of Albertine, the Proustian narrator, a little like Jake Gittes, also seeks to forget. He reminds himself of his mistakes in judgement, his pigheadedness in wanting to know the truth: did Albertine also love women? If so, who were they? Where did she meet them? Did they know each other? That summer evening, was it André who came in by the servants' entrance? Who would go with her to the racetrack in the afternoon?

Given the total impossibility of penetrating the secret of the "women in flower" the narrator in time becomes indifferent, and with age comes eventually to understand fully the vanity of his quest and the ridiculousness of his investigation:

> Suddenly my brain felt a fact that had lodged there in the guise of a memory leave its place to make room for another. The despatch that I had recently received and that I had thought came from Albertine was from Gilberte. Since the rather factitious originality of Gilberte's handwriting consisted principally in placing, in the line above

the line she was writing, the crosses on her *t*'s, making them look as if they were underlining the words higher up, or making the dots on her *i*'s look as if they were breaks in the sentences of the line above, and on the other hand to insert in the lines below the tails and the curlicues of the words that were written above, it was natural enough that a telegraph clerk should have read the scrolls of the *s*'s or the *y*'s of the upper line as a final '*ine*' closing the name of Gilberte. The dot on the *i* of Gilberte had ridden up to make a dash. As for her *G*, it had the appearance of an *A* in Gothic script. The fact that in addition to this, two or three words had been misread, entangled as they were (besides, I myself had found some incomprehensible), was enough to explain the details of my error, and it was not even necessary. How many characters in each word does a person read when his mind is on other things and when he is already sure that he knows who the letter is from. How many words in each sentence? We guess as we read, we invent; everything stems from one initial error; those that follow (and this not only in reading letters and telegrams, not even only in all acts of reading), however extraordinary they may seem to someone who does not share the same starting-point, are natural enough. Thus it is that a great deal of what we believe to be true, not to mention the ultimate conclusions that, with equal perseverance and good faith, we draw from it, results from an initial misconception of the premises.[89]

And at the conclusion of the Proustian investigation, in the closing pages of *In Search of Lost Time*, Venice, the eastern city, appropriately enough marks the last stage of the voyage. Just as for Jake Gittes in *Chinatown*, the journey ends in the East. For it is in the eastern city, the city of mirages, that the narrator and the detective reach the end of their searches.

"It began as a mistake", says Bukowski, the iconic poet of the city of Los Angeles.[90]

---

[89] Marcel Proust, *The Fugitive*, trans. Peter Collier, pp. 619-20.
[90] This is the opening line of Charles Bukowski's novel *Post Office* (Los Angeles: Black Sparrow Press, 1971).

But what mistake then? Is the mistake nothing more than a beautiful *vers(e)* hidden in the fruit?[91] A *vers(e)* wedged in the heart of love and set in the heart of literature? We love what we desire and not what we see.

I tried to make sense out of it and got nowhere.

figure 29: Billy Wilder, Double Indemnity, *1944*

---

[91] The French word here is *vers*, an untranslatable pun, as in French the word means both worm and a line of poetry, a verse. (Translator's note).

Chapter IV: Fear Noir

Doubting pleases me no less than knowing.

Dante, *Inferno* XI, 93

Spring in Los Angeles is usually a dry season. This year, it is extraordinarily wet. It must be the El Niño effect.

It's been a very long time coming. The rain, that is. Unlike its jealous lover, fire, which will put paid to Los Angeles's sultry arrogance, rain in the City of Angels is rare. Discrete. Soft and wet, loving, it is the one that gives birth, while its lover, fire, violent and terrifying, is the one that destroys.

This morning, in Griffith Park in the Hollywood Hills, where the residents, rising stars, and tourists all unite in their morning run together, the statue of James Dean silently and majestically lords it over his final stage-set, an observation post on the city. No one, or almost no one, notices him anymore.

The statue blends into the panorama for which people come from afar, above all to gaze on those famous letters: HOLLYWOOD.

This morning the statue of the rebel is the color of the sky, gray-blue; rainwater runs over it. A drop falls from the arch of its brow. A fighter's Achilles heel.

All at once white fog envelops the valley. The letters disappear. Rain falls on the city. Its heroes are worn out.

figure 30: Griffith Park @2016 fdaubigny

Color # 2 *Rebel Without a Cause*, Nicholas Ray (1955)

It is the same pallor unto death that we see on the face of the young Jim Stark (James Dean), the rebellious teenager in Nicholas Ray's film. His jacket is flaming red but his face is as white as death. Death, the unfamiliar neighbor who at night prowls the quiet neighborhoods of Los Angeles. Some unidentified place at the edge of the city, at night, the young people, free spirits with half-brained ideas, play chicken in an attempt to chase away their darkest thoughts. The cars start up, charge ahead, and then one will fall into the void. Rebels without a cause.

Boy, I'm blind as a bat.

figure 31: Nicolas Ray, Rebel Without a Cause, 195

The famous scene of the cars racing evokes that tragic moment of modernity unleashed at top speed, unmanageable, uncontrollable; that precise moment when a culture enacts the present without knowing what the next day will bring. Tomorrows that by definition are a disappointment. The cry had already been voiced in the first, forward-looking scene of Fritz Lang's masterpiece, Dr. Mabuse, *in 1922. "Ah, speed, the great cannibal!"[92] But who was there to hear it?*

---

[92] See Chapter 2. The opening scene of Fritz Lang's film *Dr. Mabuse.*

figure 32: Nicholas Ray, Rebel Without a Cause, *1955*

Something uneasy in civilization was already discernible from the beginning of the twentieth century. Sigmund Freud was among the first to place it on the couch in 1929.[93] In a sped-up world, one out of control, Europe was making a head-on entrance into a novel kind of modernity.[94]

---

[93] Sigmund Freud, *Civilization and Its Discontents* (London: Penguin, 2002).
[94] See Chapter 1 of Freud's book and the work of Jean-Martin Charcot on the manifestations of the unconscious.

figure 33: Nicholas Ray, Rebel Without a Cause, *1955*

The obsession with this new culture of speed paradoxically inspired among other things the most beautiful works of art of the time. Along with Claude Monet's *The Saint Lazare Station* (1877) and the Lumière Brothers' *Arrival of a Train at La Ciotat Station* (1895) via Etienne-Jules Marey's experiments with chronophotography (1882), we can number the many references to the world of speed in *In Search of Lost Time*.

If Marcel Proust the writer lost the love of his life, Alfred Agostinelli, in a tragic airplane accident on May 30, 1914, the lost lover will be reimagined in the novel in the guise of Albertine, the person of speed and flight par excellence.

The unique passion of the writer for the modernity represented by railroads signals an interest in an expanding culture of leisure and ease of movement that was developing in France at the same time and which would reach its height after the social revolution of

1936.[95] There are many, many examples in the novel of multiple train trips that the narrator takes from Paris to Combray or Balbec, or later from Paris to Venice.

If life on a train is often perceived by Proust as a "movable feast," since on board the social comedy of the Faubourg Saint-Germain is played and replayed, the trip in a compartment is also at the root of an odd process of defamiliarization from the rhythmic measures of everyday life, the source of a disquieting plunge into the world of the fantastic.

> In the color of the [blue] cloth, it was not so much its beauty as the sheer intensity of its blueness that seemed to outshine all other colors which had ever met my eye between my birth and the moment when my drink had begun to have its effect, leaving them as drab and dull as they would have been for someone, once blind from birth, who remembers the darkness in which his days were spent before the operation that at last enabled him late in life to see color. [...] The pleasure I felt in gazing at the blue blind and in being aware that my mouth was hanging open began to lessen. I felt more mobile and made a couple of movements; I leafed through the book my grandmother had passed me and was able to attend to a page or two here and there.[96]

In this episode, contemplating the blue color of the blind plunges the narrator into a deep visual emotion. The intensity of the sensory experience leads the narrator to experiencing something like a chromatic *black hole*, which all of a sudden sets his consciousness into action, in a way rather like the descent of consciousness into Plato's cave. Moving by train thus allows the traveler to discover new truths about art and time. And yet train travel in Proust can also be the source of anxiety-provoking experiences.

> I lowered the blue blind, which let only a strip of sunlight through. But I at once saw my grandmother, as she had

[95] It was in 1936 that a political victory was achieved by the Popular Front, a radical leftist movement which won workers two weeks of paid holiday. Following that victory, an extensive culture of leisure would develop in France.
[96] Marcel Proust, *In the Shadow of Young Girls in Flower*, trans. James Grieve, pp. 231-32.

been when sitting in the train on our departure from Paris for Balbec, and when, pained at seeing me drinking beer, she had preferred not to look, to close her eyes and pretend to be asleep. I, who had been unable to endure her sufferings in the old days when my grandfather took cognac, I had inflicted this pain on her, not simply even of seeing me take, at someone else's invitation, a drink she believed disastrous for me, but I had forced her to leave me free to swill it down as I pleased; worse still, by my rages and my breathless attacks, I had forced her to help me, to recommend it, in a supreme act of resignation whose wordless, despairing image I had before my memory, her eyes closed so as not to see.[97]

Here the experience of riding on a train seems furthermore like a pathological moment. Fear overwhelms the feeling of comfort. Whether it be trains, zeppelins, telephones, photographs, kaleidoscopes (even doorbells![98]), modern technological inventions operate in Proust like so many obsessive explorations of the unknown, as well as functioning as abysses for diving into the infinite.[99] And who can forget the scene of the telephone conversation with the narrator's grandmother, so reminiscent of Pascal's terror of the infinite:[100]

And as soon as our call has rung out, in the darkness peopled with apparitions to which our ears alone are opened, a shred of sound—an abstract sound—the sound of distance suppressed—and the voice of the dear one speaks to us.

The dear ones, the voices of the dear ones speaking, are with us. But how far away they are! How often I have been unable to listen without anguish, as if, in the face of this

[97] Ibid, pp. 182-83.
[98] In Proust's novel, the doorbell signals the moment of Charles Swann's arrival for dinner and the impossibility of the narrator's receiving his mother's kiss before going to bed, putting in train the episode of the "drama of undressing."
[99] "Plonger au fond du gouffre, Enfer ou Ciel, qu'importe?/Au fond de l'Inconnu pour trouver du *nouveau!*" (To plunge to the bottom of the abyss, hell or heaven, what does it matter?/To the depths of the unknown to discover the *new!*." Charles Baudelaire, "Le Voyage," in *Les Fleurs du mal* (Paris: Gallimard, 1972), p. 166.
[100] Blaise Pascal, *Les Pensées* (Paris: Gallimard, 2004).

impossibility of seeing, without long hours of travel, the woman whose voice was so close to my ear, I could feel more acutely how illusory the effect of such intimate proximity was, and at what a distance we can be from those we love at a moment when it seems we have only to stretch out our hands to retain them. A real presence, the voice that seems so close—but is in fact miles away! But it is also a foreglimpse of an eternal separation! Many times, as I listened in this way without seeing the woman who spoke to me from so far, I have felt that the voice was crying out to me from depths from which it would never emerge again, and I have experienced the anxiety that was one day to take hold of me when a voice would return like this (alone and no longer part of a body I was never to see again) to murmur in my ear words I would dearly like to have kissed as they passed from lips forever turned to dust.[101]

Color #3 *Peur sur la ville*, Henri Verneuil (1975)

The same dread as Pascal's of the infinite is to be found in the opening scene of Henri Verneuil's noir thriller, Peur sur la ville *(released in the United States as* The Night Caller*). The opening shot of the film begins with a long take focusing on a notebook sitting near a telephone—blue. Suggesting fear noir. The phone rings and will not stop, obsessively, terrifyingly. We find a woman alone in an upper middle-class apartment on an upper-level floor of a 70s Parisian apartment tower. We can read the anguish on her face. She picks up. It's him. She realizes that her aggressor is not far off, that he is skulking, at once everywhere and nowhere. She hears him, he is a real presence, so close and yet completely invisible. Terrified, caught in a trap without an escape, she throws herself into the void. Her aggressor is quickly identified. He materializes under a mythological fake name: Minos.*

---

[101] Marcel Proust, *The Guermantes Way*, trans. Mark Treharne (New York: Penguin Books, 2002), pp. 127-28.

figure 34: Henri Verneuil, Peur sur la Ville, *1975*

Like the insatiable Furies,[102] inhabited by a black anger, Minos torments his victims with telephone calls. He always strikes where modernity seems to him most outrageous: where obscene sex appears. A participant in the war against a modernity that he deems decadent, Minos is familiar with its classics. As an avid reader of Dante's *Divine Comedy*, he imagines a similar fate for his victims: a trip through the circles of hell.

---

[102] The Furies or Erynyes were the hellish divinities in Greek mythology responsible for carrying out judgments against the guilty. Their name comes from the "fury" that they inspired.

figure 35: Henri Verneuil, Peur sur la Ville, *1975*

Out of reverence for the poet, Marcel Proust's byline on several youthful articles was the pseudonym "Marc El Dante," and references to the *Divine Comedy* are noticeably common in *In Search of Lost Time.* They begin with the opening of the novel, which establishes an analogy between a sleeping man who holds in the circles around him the order of the hours, the years, and the worlds, and then the omnipresence of social circles which reestablish the circles of Dante's Hell: as the narrator tells us concerning the little clan of the Verdurins, "'It really is,' he said, 'the lowest thing on the social ladder, Dante's last circle'."[103]

But beyond worldly references, above all it is the theme of the circles of hell of the war which comes to occupy the central part of the novel. The conflict of World War I is in fact the historical and fictional episode that forms the structural core of a large part of the story after 1913, so much so that the author decided during the

[103] Marcel Proust, *Swann's Way,* trans. Lydia Davis, p. 298.

war to rethink the entirety of his writing project by adding a new section, *Sodom and Gomorrah,* in which he would offer theories about homosexuality and Jewishness, a section that in the end reimagines the theme of hell from the Biblical texts. And while *In Search of Lost Time* cannot be classified as a war story in the strict sense of the term, the novel nevertheless bears valuable witness to the world conflict, not just the hell of those who fought at the Front but the cynicism of those who sat it out, stayed behind, like the Verdurin clan...not to mention the author himself!

In *Finding Time Again,* Proust thus evokes "The Battle of Méséglise," an episode transformed by fiction which will be reported by the character Gilberte in a letter sent to the narrator, now an old man who is ill and ailing. The passage clearly refers to the real battle of Verdun during which the loss of human life was considerable: "The battle of Méséglise lasted for more than eight months, in the course of which the Germans lost over six hundred thousand men and destroyed Méséglise, but they did not take it."[104]

If the strategic advances of the enemy are talked about in a bantering tone at the dinner parties of the fashionable social circles, especially in *The Guermantes Way,* war in Proust is not only envisioned with its potential for physical destruction in mind, but also for its power of psychic destruction, which is equally if not more terrifying.[105] A terror that, in the context of World War I, cannot be spoken.

> It was from long lines of death, and they would never go back there, that they came among us for a fleeting moment, incomprehensible to us, filling us with tenderness, with fear, and with a sense of mystery, like the dead whom we conjure up, who appear for an instant, to whom

---

[104] Marcel Proust, *Finding Time Again,* trans. Ian Patterson (London: Penguin Books, 2002), p. 64. The Battle of Verdun during World War I took place from February 21 to December 19, 1916, in the region of Verdun in Lorraine. In the combat between the French and the German armies, some 700,000 soldiers died.
[105] Pierre Bourdieu, *Language and Symbolic Power* (Cambridge: Harvard University Press, 1991).

we cannot pose questions, and who could only reply to us in any case: "You cannot imagine."[106]

To terror can also be added the absurdity of a war that overturns society's values. From the cowardice of the "shirkers" who stayed behind (Bloch, Morel, Madame Verdurin) to the sadomasochistic indulgences of the Baron de Charlus in the Saint-Germain-des-Prés brothel where Saint-Loup will lose his *Croix de Guerre*,[107] Paris during the war became the locale of all transgressions, a bit like the biblical city of Sodom, where, below the lights and outbursts of the zeppelin attacks, the final apocalypse was awaited:

> From our balcony the city, which had seemed merely a place of formless, shifting blackness, suddenly passed from the depths of night into the glowing sky, where at the shattering sound of the sirens the airmen soared up one by one, while with a slower but more insidious and alarming movement, as their questing gaze suggested the still invisible object, perhaps already close at hand, which they were seeking, the searchlights moved ceaselessly across the sky, sniffing out the enemy, surrounding him with their beams until the moment when the aeroplanes were ready to shoot off in pursuit to strike him down. And, squadron after squadron, each airman was thus soaring up above the city, transported now into the sky, like a Valkyrie. But here and there on the ground, at the level of the houses, lights went on, and I told Saint-Loup that if he had been at home the previous evening he might, while contemplating the apocalypse in the sky, have been able to see on the ground (as in El Greco's *Burial of Count Orgaz*, where these different levels are parallel) a genuine farce played out by characters in their nightshirts, all of them celebrities whose names would have been worth sending to a successor of Ferrari, whose Society Notes had so often entertained Saint-Loup and myself that we used to amuse ourselves by making up imaginary ones. And that is what we did again that day, as

---

[106] Marcel Proust, *A La recherche du temps perdu*, ed. Jean-Paul Tadié, Esquisse IX, tome 4, p. 774. (Translation by BW).

[107] The *Croix de Guerre* (1915-1918) was a military decoration given to recognize a commander's citation of a soldier for outstanding conduct during World War I.

if there were no war on, even though the subject, the fear of Zeppelins, was very "wartime."[108]

The episode develops almost like a scene in a movie. From the movement of the light-beams seeking out the enemy, to the operatic ballet of the zeppelins by way of the piercing noise of the sirens, the scene evokes a modern black epic poem closer to Francis Ford Coppola's *Apocalypse Now* (1979) than to a novel, as Céline said, replete with "people of the void, ghosts of desires, irresolute old roués awaiting their Watteau moment."[109]

While it is true that Proust did not go to fight at the Front as many of his contemporaries did (Roland Dorgelès, Blaise Cendrars, or even Guillaume Apollinaire)—the writer was considered ineligible because of his terrible bouts of asthma—from his room at the Ritz and his apartment on Boulevard Haussmann, Proust will remain a privileged witness of the casualties of war, recreating with exactitude its anxiety-ridden character.

For if *In Search of Lost Time* has often been classified as a story of initiation, it remains nevertheless a gloomy story of cloistering and closeting. Closed and closeted spaces (rooms) are common, and an entire volume, *The Prisoner*, hinges upon a story of physical and psychological confinement.[110]

While the episodes of the war and of the death of Alfred Agostinelli first disrupt and then change the structure of the novel after 1913, the parts devoted to Albertine (*The Prisoner* and *The Fugitive*) consecrate the themes of jealousy and confinement. *The Prisoner* forms a masterly description of a darkening of consciousness, divided into six nights, during which the narrator, in the dark room of his obsessions, forges the instruments of self-torture by imagining Albertine deserting him for other women.

In this bleak part of the novel, perhaps the bleakest and the *noirest,* the pace of jealousy reflects the narrator's psychological

---

[108] Marcel Proust, *Finding Time Again*, trans. Ian Patterson, pp. 66-67.
[109] Louis-Ferdinand Céline, *Voyage au bout de la nuit* [Voyage to the End of Night] (Paris: Denoël et Steele, 1932), p. 93. (Translation by BW)
[110] See Chapter 1. See also the "rooms" of Michel Butor.

need to make excuses. What's to be done? Marry Albertine or leave her and take off for Venice? The question gets repeated. There is no clear answer, just gloomy alternatives.

Jealousy, as a well-known psychological state, exists in Proust in a somewhat different dimension, especially if we are proposing to re-read the novel as a *noir* fiction. Much more than being an affective and emotional syndrome, jealousy is also connected to a space where the fascinatory gaze is diffracted. The author Robbe-Grillet will later exploit the theme of "jalousie" in its other meaning of a Venetian blind through which it is possible to see without being seen.[III] A new question arises: does the Proustian narrator foreshadow the theme of the detective as a voyeur?

> On the point of knocking on the shutters, he felt a pang of shame thinking that Odette was going to know he had been suspicious, that he had come back, that he had posted himself in the street. She had often told him what a horror she had of jealous men, of lovers who spied. What he was about to do was very uncouth, and from now on she would detest him, whereas now, for the moment, so long as he had not knocked, perhaps, even while deceiving him, she loved him. How often we sacrifice the fulfillment of a possible happiness to our impatience for an immediate pleasure! But the desire to know the truth was stronger and seemed to him nobler. He knew that the reality of certain circumstances which he would have given his life to reconstruct accurately could be read behind that window striated with light, as under the gold-illuminated cover of one of those precious manuscripts to whose artistic richness itself the scholar who consults them cannot remain indifferent. He felt a delicious pleasure in learning the truth that so impassioned him from this unique, ephemeral, and precious transcript, made of a translucid substance so warm and so beautiful. Then, too, the advantage he felt he had—that he so needed to feel he had—over them lay perhaps less in knowing than in being able to show them he knew. He raised himself on his tiptoes. He knocked. They had not heard, he knocked again more loudly, the conversation stopped. A

[III] Alain Robbe-Grillet, *Jalousie* (Paris: Minuit, 1957).

man's voice which he tried to distinguish from among the voices of those of Odette's friends whom he knew asked:

"Who's there?"[112]

figure 36: David Lynch, Blue Velvet, *1986*

Color #4 *Blue Velvet*, David Lynch (1986)

Who's there? Who's there was that somber man dressed in yellow come for that night to visit Dorothy Vallens (Isabella Rossellini) in her intensely blue apartment. As he spies on a violent nighttime encounter through the slats of a closet, young Jeffrey Beaumont (Kyle MacLachlan), anti-hero of this very *noir* film by David Lynch, strangely resembles Charles Swann, the outlandish dandy in love with Odette, the woman with a thousand faces of *In Search of Lost Time,* in love and well on his way to self-destruction. Is the lover a perverse beast? He who forms the beauty forms the beast. The old tale is well known. The inescapable need for knowing at all costs the truth about Dorothy will lead Swann and Jeffrey not down the way to truth but rather down the path of their own demons.

---

[112] Marcel Proust, *Swann's Way,* trans. Lydia Davis, pp. 284-85.

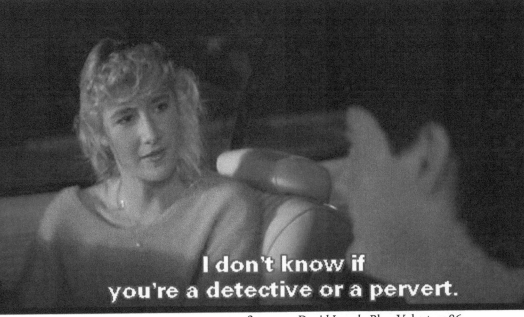

figure 37: David Lynch, Blue Velvet, *1986*

"Are you a detective or a pervert?," Jeffrey's girlfriend Nancy asks.

"This is what I will find out," he replies, unsure of the response he will discover.

The crime is not always where you imagine it to be. The beast slumbers in us.

From the theatre of the Roussainville forest where the Proustian narrator, without being seen, watches the sexual revels of Mlle de Venteuil to the Parisian brothel where he is a voyeur, through the bull's eye, spying on the sadomasochistic pleasures of the Baron de Charlus—in the Proustian novel the Venetian blind unendingly reveals a dramatic and poetic space in which a complex fantasmagoria of desire is deployed, one analogous to the aesthetic of film noir.

For film noir is not only a thematic classification; it harks back to a well-established visual aesthetic that certain critics have not shrunk from terming "sensual." Through the use of strong lighting contrasts, off-kilter framing, vertical or horizontal, voice-overs and flash-backs, the visual techniques of film noir are astonishingly similar to the visual poetics of the Proustian novel.[113]

From the shadows cast on the secret lives of the "young girls in flower," to the geometrical framing of blinds, by way of the long take on Albertine's beauty mark, the technique of flash-back in *In Search*, of all available narrative techniques, is one of the most heavily used.

For example, in *The Fugitive* there are numerous narrative flash-backs, where they imitate the anxious narrator's route as he inquires into Albertine's troubled past; it is as though the narrator, searching for truth, needed like a detective to revamp the hypotheses of the preceding day because they never line up perfectly with the current facts of a being always one step ahead of him.

And in his use of the technique of the voice-over, when the voice of the adult narrator is imposed over the voice of the young narrator, once again Proust is being innovative by expanding a little further the visual, narrative, and resonant limits of the traditional novel. The episode in which the young Marcel and the aging Baron de Charlus meet at the seaside in *In the Shadow of Young Girls in Flower* is a masterpiece. The scene, recounted on one level by an innocent young man who is manifestly ignorant of the Baron's homosexuality, is enriched by the implicit comments of the adult narrator, who understands the Baron's preference for young boys.

> He had drawn himself up with a challenging air, setting
> his lips in a sneer, twirling his mustache, and charging his
> eye with something hard and indifferent, something
> close to insulting. It was the strangeness of his expression
> that made me think he must be a thief, if not a madman.
> Yet his way of dressing, which was the acme of good taste,
> was both much more serious and much more simple than

---

[113] Denise Warren, "Out of the Past: Semiotic Configurations of the Femme Fatale in Film Noir," *Interdisciplinary Journal of German Linguistics and Semiotic Analysis* 2, 2 (Fall 1997), pp. 221-55.

that of any of the bathers I saw at Balbec, as well as being something of a comfort to me in my suit, which had so often been humiliated by the bright and banal whiteness of their beach outfits. [...] His glance flashed rapidly through me just as before; then, as though he had not seen me, it lowered, seemed to settle somewhere outside his eyes, dull and neutral, like a look that feigns to see nothing outside itself, and is incapable of seeing anything inside, the look expressing nothing but the satisfaction of knowing it is edged by eyelashes, among which it merely sits, roundly pleased with its own crass candor, the smug and sanctimonious look of certain hypocrites, the con-ceited look of certain fools. I saw that he had changed his clothes: the suit he now wore was even darker than the other one—no doubt true elegance is closer to simplicity than is false elegance, but there was something else about him: at close range, one sensed that the almost complete absence of color from his clothes came not from any in-difference to color, but because, for some reason, he deprived himself of it. The sobriety apparent in his cloth-ing gave the impression of deriving from a self-imposed diet, rather than from any lack of appetite. In the fabric of his trousers, a fine stripe of dark green harmonized with a line visible in his socks, the refinement of this touch revealing the intensity of a preference which, though suppressed everywhere else, had been tolerated in that one form as a special concession, whereas a red design in the cravat remained as imperceptible as a lib-erty not quite taken, a temptation not quite succumbed to.[114]

Beneath the lack of color of the somber suit, which one imagines as black and white, the variegated accessories burst out. Under the pavement, the beach. Behind the darkness of convention, the rev-olution in manners. From the Proustian story, which threads the needle, emerges a color revolution at the turn of the century. So too with black and white film which, evolving from silent to talky, foreshadows the premises of a technicolor revolution.

---

[114] Marcel Proust, *In the Shadow of Young Girls in Flower*, trans. James Grieve, pp. 333-34.

Noir #8 FINAL CUT *Out of the Past*, Jacques Tourneur (1947)

In a scene from French director Jacques Tourneur's film Out of the
Past *(1947), shot in Los Angeles, Jeff Markham (Robert Mitchum),
driving his pick-up truck, tells his friend Ann about his past as a detective and his fatal passion for the beautiful Kathie Moffat (Jane
Greer).*

figure 38: *Jacques Tourneur,* Out of the Past, *1947*

*While Jeff avows that he has turned the page on his past, the dou-
bling up of two narrative voices using voice-over points to how the
drama of memory is unresolved and exists in a suspended state. A
work in progress. Jeff's story will continue throughout the night. To
the end of the film. A bit like Céline, who both admired and loathed
Proust.*[115] *The film* Out of the Past *evolves into a story of uninter-
rupted memory and carries on into the dawn. A little in the style of*

---

[115] See note 18.

those oriental tales in A Thousand and One Nights, *the telling of which continue forever out of a fear that their conclusion portends death.*

A Thousand and One Nights. The awakening of consciousness. Going out with him right from the first night, Scheherazade already understood everything. Seduction, death, the moment of the crime. In a word, she knew she was going to die. Only one thing could save her. Telling her story. To the very end of night.

figure 39: Billy Wilder, Double Indemnity, *1944*

EPILOGUE
(The Long Goodbye)[116]

For Roland Barthes, the farewell to his mother comprised a small book made up of a series of photographs. A project begun in the darkroom out of which came the clarity of his *Camera Lucida.*[117]

A sort of dive into the night of memories to bring into the sunshine the light shed by a love.

Camera Lucida was Roland Barthes's last essay, published a little after the death of his mother in 1977 and shortly before his own death, following a tragic vehicular accident, on March 26, 1980.

The French semiotician's book of notes on photography was originally a project commissioned by the editor Jean Narboni for the series "Night Will Be Black and White" in the journal *Cahiers du Cinéma.* Concerning film Barthes at first replied that he had nothing to say and, as for photography, maybe...[118] Something like *beside the point/beside the (photographic) plate.*

Among all of Roland Barthes's essays, *Camera Lucida* is considered the most Proustian, in its themes of memory and childhood, and in the particular attention brought to bear in poetic detail (*punctum*) which, with the instant of the photograph, makes the objective image (*studium*) topple into the subjective fiction. In Barthes, the smallest detail functions like that little patch of yellow wall in Vermeer's painting which the writer Bergotte, in *In Search of Lost Time,* saw only a few minutes before his death, thus creating a fault line between what the viewer knows and what he sees *according to his own desire.*[119]

---

[116] The reference is to Robert Altman's film *The Long Goodbye* (1973), adapted from Raymond Chandler's 1953 novel of the same title.

[117] Roland Barthes, *Camera Lucida: On Photography,* trans. Richard Howard (London: Vintage, 2000).

[118] Louis-Jean Calvet, *Roland Barthes, 1915-1980* (Paris: Flammarion, 2014), p. 281.

[119] See Chapter 2.

figure 40: Johannes Vermeer, View of Delft, 1660-1661

Roland Barthes's study of photography is fascinating in the sense that at the outset it proposes a misunderstanding. Not to respond exactly to the problem posed to him: a question of cinema. Like a diversion from the dutiful investigation. By paying little attention to the initial subject, it offers permission to wander poetically, a permission which progressively yields to intellectual rambling. By overturning the ecology of the traditional essay, Barthes reveals a new fault-line between what constitutes truth and falsehood, academic commentary and personal fiction.

This is exactly the literary geology, from Montaigne to Barthes, that I proposed to follow in my essay *Proust in Black (Los Angeles: A Proustian Fiction)*. It too proposed a commentary *beside the point/beside the plate*. In this essay, I have attempted to push, side-step, and upend the anchor points of traditional academic discourse on the Proustian novel and film noir by making them collide. So as better to bear witness to a theoretical disaster over the fault-line, here in Los Angeles, at the edge of the Pacific. The disaster which is at issue in this essay on *writing black* takes multiple forms. It is the reaction, immediate and deferred, to several semantic shocks.

Balanced between two centuries, two continents, two modes of thought and two modes of writing, this experimental essay with fictional alliances stages a double desire: the desire for knowledge and the desire for writing.

The desire to go on to confession.

Farewell to a black and white world, farewell to the traditional essay, farewell to a *certain kind* of literature, and farewell to a *certain* love. To return writing to its central place, *to essay* (in the verbal sense) a different tack.

Marlowe never sleeps 'till all is well in the world

Raymond Chandler

figure 41 opposite: Griffith Park, at noon @2016 fdaubigny

Translator's Afterword

Bruce Whiteman

In this year 2019, exactly a century after Marcel Proust controversially won the Prix Goncourt for *À L'ombre des jeunes filles en fleurs*, the second volume of *À La recherche du temps perdu,* Proust's presence in literary culture remains as strong as ever. There exists a formidable library of books about the French writer, ranging from readers' guides to scholarly studies, even to books that mine Proust for moral guidance, for cuisine, for visual art, and of course for music (the famous "little phrase" which has so fascinated musical readers). Proust's English readership widened enormously with the fresh translations of all seven volumes of his novel that came out in the early 2000s, the first retranslation since the Scott Moncrieff version of the 1920s and 1930s. Like the Septuagint and the King James Bible, it required a team of translators, and it was widely and enthusiastically reviewed.

But even amidst a river of books that threatens to drown the most devoted Proustian, Fanny Daubigny's *Proust in Black* is startlingly unique. She has collocated two phenomena, what she calls "two heterogeneous artistic elements"—Proust, who died in 1922, and film noir, which we tend to think of as belonging most enduringly to the 1940s and 1950s—and she has created a kind of experimental essay that at heart is based not in scholarship but in the imagination. Daubigny was born and raised in France but has lived in Los Angeles for many years. L.A. is, of course, the epicenter of film noir, not just the site where the studios and their directors created the movies, but the actual location for many of film noir's most canonical scenes and stories. Daubigny finds the crucial characteristics of the genre everywhere in Proust's novel: the omnipresence of night and dreams and shadows, the haunting nature of memory, the *femmes fatales* through whose dark egoism and secret agendas the stories inescapably lead to destruction and death. Los Angeles in turn acquires a Proustian cast, haunted by history and haunted by love. It is where Daubigny takes on "conscience, truth, desire and modernity" like a symbolic gumshoe, tracing them in Proust and also finding them everywhere in the films she explores, from a Buster Keaton silent film from 1924 in which he plays an aspiring detective and a film projectionist, to films by Roman Polanski and David Lynch that are among the "noirest" of the film noir genre.

I see *Proust in Black* as falling not so much into the French tradition of the *essai* but as belonging more to that special strain of Anglo-American literary criticism in which the author takes no pains to hide her face, but in fact celebrates the individual imagination as it exuberantly confronts a text of deeply personal significance. I am thinking of books like Henry Miller's *Time of the Assassins* and Charles Olson's *Call Me Ishmael*.

These books and others like them eschew the objectivity of academic scholarship and seek instead to shed light on the texts they have chosen through imaginative indirection, personal investment, and poetry. In her short book, Daubigny brings her two obsessions together and looks at them through a complex lens, through two narratives, really, citing not just some of the great noir films and the Proustian novel and its

allied texts (*Contre Sainte Beuve* and *Jean Santeuil*), but visual art, photography, Keats, Dante, Rimbaud, Robbe-Grillet, Freud, and much more.

She calls her book "a brief archaeology," but perhaps she means that more in the nineteenth-century than in the Foucauldian sense. Or perhaps it is Roland Barthes who needs to be named here, since in *Proust in Black* it is Barthes's *Camera Lucida* that Daubigny summons as a parallel to her own preoccupation: "A sort of deep dive into the night of memories to being into the sunshine the light shed by a love."

The heart of Proust's *roman-fleuve* is undeniably laid bare by the writer-as-detective-as-archaeologist in a novel and compelling way—it "essays a different tack," to cite the book's final words. In doing so it creates its own dark and haunting text, a portrait "in black" perhaps reminiscent of the black border of Victorian letter-paper meant for notes of consolation following a death. Lost time, "the black hole of history" as Daubigny calls it, can only be reimagined in black and white: the black and white of film and the black and white of type on paper in deeply imaginative books.

Bruce Whiteman is a poet, translator, and reviewer. His most recent book is a collection of prose poems entitled The Sad Mechanic Exercise. *He teaches at the University of Toronto and is the poet in residence at Scattergood Friends School in West Branch, Iowa. He lives most of the year in Toronto.*

About the Author

Fanny Daubigny is a French-born, Los Angeles–based writer, poet, and translator. She teaches French and Francophone Literatures at California State University, Fullerton, where she serves as Professor of French in the Department of Modern Languages and Literatures. She has published numerous articles on Marcel Proust and is a specialist in French and French literatures of the nineteenth and twentieth century.